Creating a Learning Environment for
Babies & Toddlers

Creating a Learning Environment for
Babies & Toddlers

Ann Clare

Los Angeles | London | New Delhi
Singapore | Washington DC

First published 2012

SAGE Publications Ltd
1 Oliver's Yard
55 City Road
London EC1Y 1SP

SAGE Publications Inc.
2455 Teller Road
Thousand Oaks, California 91320

SAGE Publications India Pvt Ltd
B 1/I 1 Mohan Cooperative Industrial Area
Mathura Road
New Delhi 110 044

SAGE Publications Asia-Pacific Pte Ltd
3 Church Street
#10-04 Samsung Hub
Singapore 049483

Library of Congress Control Number: 2011931793

British Library Cataloguing in Publication data

A catalogue record for this book is available from the British Library

ISBN 978-0-85702-768-9
ISBN 978-0-85702-769-6

Typeset by C&M Digitals (P) Ltd, Chennai, India
Printed and bound by CPI Group (UK) Ltd, Croydon, CR0 4YY (for Antony Rowe)
Printed on paper from sustainable resources

MIX
Paper from
responsible sources
FSC   FSC® C013604
www.fsc.org

Contents

Acknowledgements

I came into the field of early years relatively late in my career, but ever since I arrived I have had the pleasure of working with and knowing some of the most skilled professionals in this area. I would like to take this opportunity of thanking them for giving me enjoyment in my work. Two of them, Cathy Nutbrown and Jools Page, I thank for giving me confidence and a belief in myself.

The support I have received from my editor, Jude Bowen, has been amazing and I thank her for putting up with me.

My thanks go to all those who engaged with me by letting me observe their children and to Rachel and Sam I give special thanks for letting me into their lives.

My original interest in young children came from three very special and inspirational people, Felicity, Edward and Hannah, and this is continuing through Oscar. I thank them and continue to be inspired by them.

About the Author

Ann Clare, PhD is an Early Years Foundation Stage consultant working for Trafford Children and Young People's Service. Ann originally qualified as a secondary school English teacher, before studying for her MA in Early Childhood Education whilst running a small nursery. She also has experience of working as an area manager for a private day nursery chain, and has been an assessor for the Early Years Professional Status. After working for several years in another north-west local authority, Ann decided to conduct her own research with children under the age of 3 in out-of-home care settings, as part of her journey towards gaining her PhD at the University of Sheffield. Ann now supports students studying for their MA in Early Childhood Education at the University of Sheffield. Her main area of interest within the field of early years is babies and young children under the age of 3. She has written two articles for an early years magazine on this subject, and this is her first book.

List of Figures

Why Environments Matter

This chapter will:

- consider the increased importance given to the care and education of young children in recent years
- discuss the importance of early environments
- look at the provision made for this care and education across the UK
- introduce some of the children and settings used in the case studies.

Throughout recent history, the pioneers of early childhood education have very much focused their ethos and philosophy around children over 3 years of age, and as a result much research conducted has concentrated on these years. It has almost appeared as if society does not place value on any learning that has taken place in the first three years of life. This lack of evidence and research was recognized by David et al. (2003, p. 9) in the literature review for the *Birth to Three Matters* framework (DfES, 2002):

> [There is] a paucity of evidence about processes and practices in ECEC for children from birth to three years. In particular the field needs research information about toddlers in educare settings, as well as that exploring the impact of practitioner training on the experiences of children and parents. (David et al., 2003, p. 9)

This quotation demonstrates that research for the under 3s has long been neglected and, for me, it was one of the starting points for my own personal research. Having worked in a range of settings in two north-west local authorities for over 10 years, it became evident to me that the quality of the environment available to a baby or a young child was vitally important in its learning, development and wellbeing. I decided to investigate different early environments, and the practices of the adults working with children and babies under 3 in these environments.

The importance of environments

The importance that the development of children under 3 has gained in status over recent years has increasingly become the driving force behind some political initiatives (Field, 2010; Allen, 2011). Rightly, the development that children make in their early years is recognized as the precursor of future good outcomes.

With this and my own personal involvement of accessing private day care for my oldest daughter, I decided to conduct some research into the experiences of babies and children under the age of 3 in out-of-home settings, and the implications that this had for the adults involved. This book will draw on the case studies that emerged from the research I conducted, and on my own professional experiences of working within two local authorities. Throughout this book, there are case studies to illustrate the different experiences, relationships and environments that babies and young children are offered and affected by. The following detailed case study clearly identifies the themes of the book.

Case study 1: Observation of a mother and baby playing together

- Mum places 4-month-old Oscar on the blanket on his tummy. She lays in front of him, talking to him and trying to engage him in some eye contact. As she talks, she gently touches his hand.
- The tone of her voice is gentle and soothing.
- She calls Oscar by his name, asking him if he would like to roll over for her like he did yesterday. As he does not respond, she asks him if he is too tired. She refers to the rolling over as 'his new trick'.
- He pulls himself up fully on his hands and looks around. He begins to make babbling sounds as Mum still talks to him. She talks to him about yesterday when he rolled over three times in a row. She reinforces the pleasure that this has given her by saying, 'Such a clever boy'. Mum then asks, 'Are you going to go on your back?', as he begins to demonstrate by the sounds that he is making that he has had enough time on his tummy.

- She asks him what he wants to do instead, as she pulls him up on to his feet, talking to him all of the time and maintaining eye contact with him.
- As she lays him down on his back, she says, 'Down we go'. Oscar looks as his feet so Mum asks, 'Are these your feet? Do they belong to you?' He babbles and begins to smile in response. (Mum knows that he has a previous interest in his feet.)
- Mum bends over him saying, 'Would you like to play with these? Shall we sing a little song?' As she holds him by the feet, she begins to sing, 'Roly, poly up, roly, poly down, roly poly ever so slowly, roly poly up', moving his feet in time with the rhythm of the music up and down in the air. All through this episode, she maintains eye contact and Oscar responds by bursting out with loud giggles and starts to move his arms more vigorously. Mum asks him if it is his favourite song and shall she do it again? When he does not respond in the same manner, she suggests that they do another song, Wind the Bobbin Up, not with his hands but with his feet again. Oscar is still engaged with his mother.
- She pulls him up to her and then places him down, and notices that he has focused on a caterpillar which she refers to as Colin. She suggests that Oscar tells Colin about his holidays. 'What did you do on your holidays, Oscar?' She pauses and then supplies his response, 'Did you go the aquarium? Did you see lots of fishes? Which were your favourite fishes? Are you going to tell Colin about your favourite fishes? Or are your favourite fishes at home?' All through this interaction she pauses, waiting for response.
- Oscar puts his fingers in his mouth and Mum warns him, 'Don't put those fingers too far back. We know what happens when you put them too far back, you sometimes get sick'.
- Mum notices that he has begun to focus on a photograph, and so she follows this by saying, 'Are you looking at the picture of mummy and daddy? Is that what you are looking at? They don't look like that any more. That was a long time ago. It's in Japan, you would like it in Japan because there are lots of bright lights there. You like the bright lights, don't you?' Oscar responds by babbling in the pauses. She goes on to comment, 'There aren't many photographs of mummy and daddy left now as they have all been replaced by you'. As she says this, she bends down to kiss him.

This short observation of just over 6 minutes gives a wealth of rich information which is worthy of detailed examination. This natural observation of the play interaction between mother and child epitomizes the environment that we would all like to create for the babies and young children in our care. The positive learning that is taking place in this case study clearly illustrates the strong bond between mother and child; both of them feel comfortable in each other's company. The mother has created an atmosphere of peace and calm and gives her son her undivided attention. He is in an environment with which he is familiar; it is not overcrowded by toys or bombarded by external noises. It is quiet, cosy and comfortable. The mother reads Oscar's signals well, responding to them as she changes his position but still endeavouring to maintain eye contact and sustain his interest. As she gains this contact, she chooses to sing a rhyme with which he is familiar and which is much loved. She knows that he likes his feet, so she uses these to do the actions. As she goes through the actions, Oscar responds by increasing his arm movements and by giggling with delight, letting her know that he is enjoying this and that his levels of wellbeing are high. Again, the mother follows his lead, noticing where his eyes are focused on Colin, a favourite companion, and so she suggests that Oscar tells him about his holiday and the fishes that he has seen. Here the mum is making links for the baby between his experiences, talking about the fish in the aquarium and the fish that Oscar likes to watch at home. When his attention focuses on a photograph, she comments on this and again links it to his experiences. This is his daddy. Japan is a place of bright lights, something which he likes. Again, the mother places these subjects within Oscar's experiences and interests.

In our day care settings, we need to ask ourselves if we create an environment such as this for the babies and young children in our care. I would suggest that as practitioners we are more concerned with what the aesthetic of the environment is like rather than how the environment can nurture. We are more concerned with the 'care' as opposed to the learning. Frequently, the environments for the very youngest of our children are made to look like the environments that I would expect to see for children of 3 years or more, which is completely inappropriate. The environment has to nurture the baby and young child, to make her feel safe and secure, to enable her to form attachments and to give her the opportunity to make links with her experiences. It is only when these things are in place that the babies and young children in our care will grow and develop emotionally, cognitively and physically.

The environment is the place where we as human beings conduct our research. As Gopnik et al. (2001, p. 158) rightly assert:

> That leaves us free to explore many possibilities and to learn just what to do in our particular world. Childhood is a time when we can safely devote ourselves to learning about our specific physical and social environment. We can do pure basic research.

This research through engagement with our environments enables the brain to make connections and so aid learning. Environments for very young children should not just be clean and 'pretty looking' – they should be places of exploration, excitement and most importantly love.

The different threads of attachment, wellbeing, involvement, inter-action, physical environment and knowledge of parents will all be unravelled in the following chapters.

Policy makers and the environment

It is clear from the publication of reports (Field, 2010; Allen, 2011; Tickell, 2011) that policy makers are alerting society to the importance of the first two years of life. These reports clearly identify that the first two years are key to the future development of an individual. It is for this reason that there are now initiatives which are targeting the vulnerable in our society though the children's centre programme which is becoming less of a universal service and more about the funding of these children taking places in care settings when they reach 2 years old. I would question the removal of the universal offer because parenting problems can occur any time and anywhere: a concern is that this becomes a form of crisis management for parents, mothers in particular.

Policy makers are directing initiatives with a focus on the home learning environment as discussed in *Opening Doors, Breaking Barriers: A Strategy for Social Mobility* (HM Government, 2011):

> ... the home learning environment is the most important factor in children's cognitive and social and behaviour outcomes. In the early years, a strong home environment is characterized by activities such as talking and reading to children, singing songs and learning through simple activities and play.

This therefore is the type of environment that babies and young children should have access to within our day care provision if we are to continue to support all babies and children to achieve their potential both cognitively and emotionally.

Theorists

There are two theorists, Vygotsky and Piaget, whose thinking is useful to look at when examining the case study described earlier. It can be used to clearly illustrate Vygotsky's (1978) theory of the zone of proximal development (ZPD), which he describes as the way in which children have their learning scaffolded by others, their peers and knowledgeable adults, are influenced by what they already know and can do, and are within a particular society/culture at a moment in time, in order that they can move forwards. Oscar is undoubtedly having his learning scaffolded by his mother, as she models language and interaction for him. She makes links to things which he already knows and can do, such as his awareness of fish and his ability to roll over. The mother also places Oscar within the culture of his nuclear family by talking about his holidays, the fish at home, his father and the life that they had before they became parents. This close link to the theories of Vygotsky is not evidenced when we relate this case study to Piaget's theories of child development. Central to Piaget's thinking about a child's development are the steps that he said all babies and young children go through as they develop.

The four development stages are described in Piaget's theory as:

- Sensorimotor stage: from birth to age 2 (children experience the world through movement and senses and learn object permanence)
- Preoperational stage: age 2 to 7 (acquisition of motor skills)
- Concrete operational stage: age 7 to 11 (children begin to think logically about concrete events)
- Formal operational stage: after age 11 (development of abstract reasoning).

Piaget saw these stages as sequential, in that each child will go through the stages in order without missing any out. Piaget felt that children under the age of 7 are not social in their verbal interactions and in their play. He notes 'the absence of any sustained social intercourse between the children of less than 7 or 8 ...' (Piaget, 1959, p. 40) and that 'Up till the age of about 5, the child almost always works alone' (p. 41). Clearly, the case study demonstrates the interaction that Oscar is engaging in with his mother at the age of only 4 months.

The case studies used throughout this book will challenge the latter statement as they describe children initially playing alongside, and then beginning to actively engage in social play with, their peers and siblings. Piaget's studies have been criticized as more recent research (Burman, 1994; James et al., 1998) has emerged challenging his theories because he studied children's development through the laboratory rather than looking at how children interact with their environment, their peers and others.

Vygotsky, on the other hand, believed in the importance of adult support and interaction in structuring children's learning. In this respect, Vygotsky differed from Piaget (1959) when he states:

> His [Piaget's] conception of the development of thought is based on the premise taken from psychoanalysis that the child's thought is originally and naturally autistic and becomes realistic thought only under long and sustained social pressure. (Vygotsky, 1986, p. 18)

Unlike Piaget, Vygotsky believed that it is a child's interaction with society and with others that enables him to develop. Piaget's child has to lose 'his' egocentric nature before 'he' can use social interaction as a driver for development, which is the opposite of Vygotsky (1986).

The present day

Many of the ideas, visions and theoretical thinking of the pioneers and theorists resonate in the political agenda of today, which is a challenging thought. How far have we come in the last hundred or so years if we are still legislating to pull children out of poverty, and if we are still questioning the quality of provision that we are providing for babies and young children? The introduction of the EYFS, the *Early Years Foundation Stage*, in England (DfES, 2007) gave early years practitioners a principled approach to follow with babies and young children experiencing out-of-home care, but we are still facing a political agenda which is looking to practitioners to meet targets and to achieve immediate successes, rather than perhaps taking a more visionary view on how these principles might impact on the future lives of these children. At the time of writing, we face a further challenge in a period of recession, one where many politicians have seen the work of the EYFS (DfES, 2007) as having been to create a 'nappy' curriculum, especially in relation to children under 3 years of age. It remains to be seen if we will return to an earlier place in history where the learning and needs of children under 3 were seen as secondary to those of children over 3. Are we perhaps in danger of losing all of the skills, especially of childminders and practitioners in day nurseries, acquired during the last 10 years?

Across the UK, there are a range of frameworks to support the care and learning of babies and young children. In England at the time of writing, the EYFS (DfES, 2007) has just been reviewed and the report published (Tickell, 2011). There are a range of recommendations which may have an impact on the way in which the curriculum is offered in the future. Two of these recommendations are:

- the development of key milestones for the development of children under 24 months
- the strengthening of the links between health and learning where parents and carers can contribute to a child's early childhood record (known as the Red Book).

In Scotland, for babies and children under 3 there is *Pre-Birth to Three* (The Scottish Government, 2010) which recognizes that a baby's learning takes place from conception – not just the natural physical development but also the important bonding and relationship-building that occurs throughout pregnancy. This is the only one of the home countries which recognizes the importance of the pregnancy months in the future learning and development of children.

Like Scotland, Wales has two approaches to supporting children in the early years. The Welsh *Early Years Foundation Phase* is to support children aged 3 to 8 and is statutory, and there is the Flying Start programme for the 0–3-year age group.

Like England, at the time of writing, the Northern Ireland early years strategy 0–6 is under review. In the Republic of Ireland, there is a loose curriculum – Aistear (2010) – for children from birth to 6 years. Interestingly, this is optional and within it there is an emphasis on practitioners interpreting it in line with their own skills and knowledge.

Maternity leave and parental choice

Mothers today are offered a year's maternity leave from their employment, which means that frequently babies are not accessing out-of-home day care provision until they are much older, which many practitioners believe causes more problems when it comes to separation. Practitioners often comment on how it is more difficult to settle babies when they are older, as they experience more anxiety at separation than when they were a few months old. This is in line with the thinking of Bowlby (1989) and Ainsworth (1969) when they conducted their research into attachment theory.

As well as having access to longer periods of maternity leave, parents are also offered a plethora of choices when it comes to choosing childcare, which are frequently influenced by economic factors. Most childcare today is expensive, and many parents prefer to leave their baby with someone who is known to them. This role is increasingly taken up by grandparents who, after having cared for their own children, are now caring for their children's children, with an impact on the age and quality of their retirement. If a family carer cannot be used, parents of young children have to choose between full day care and childminders

Case study settings and children

As they will appear throughout the book, the babies and children that I observed need to be introduced, and a description provided of the various settings they attended. When I first decided to conduct the research, a day nursery in the local authority where I worked was asked if contact could be made with their parents to gain permission to interview them and then to observe and photograph their children until they reached 3 years of age. The staff in the nursery were also asked if they would take part in interviews, so that an understanding of their perspectives could be gained. The initial response was poor, but I was able to go ahead and carry out the research with the children of 11 parents who had agreed to take part. At the same time, a colleague of mine, who was expecting her third baby, agreed that her child could be observed as she stayed at home to bring him up. Although the observation of this baby was not the driving force of my research, it ultimately became very important to me, not just for my research but personally, as Sam has become an important part of my life.

As the research continued, I was able to increase the number of children and families involved by recruiting another day nursery to join the study. A further three children for the research were recruited in this way. The two nurseries were completely different in the way in which they were run, and the addition of the second nursery ultimately proved to be fortuitous in the way that it contributed to the findings from the study, and in particular to the research study of the baby brought up at home by his mother.

The first day nursery

The first nursery was privately owned, and was established in 2002. It was fairly new at the time of the research study. This newness of environment and resources was one of the many reasons why parents chose it. It was situated near to a main arterial road network, which was another reason why many parents had chosen to attend this setting, in a leafy suburban area. The building was old, and it had its own car park; there was a small hard-core outdoor area for the older children, and a small area of artificial grass for the 18-month-to 2-year-olds. The outdoor area was accessible from two of the downstairs rooms, and this was another one of the stated reasons for some parents' choice of setting. The nursery was divided into five rooms, and the children moved from room to room according to their chronological age, with the exception of the move from the baby room to the toddler room, where the babies moved according to the confidence in their mobility. There were 68 children under 5 years of age attending this nursery. The setting had 11 staff, and the proprietor was also the manager. When asked why they had chosen this setting over others, two sets of parents said that their child had previously been to another setting; the reason for the move had been the establishing of this nursery near to where they lived and for another parent it was due to her experience of that previous setting:

> It [the first setting chosen] seemed OK. When I first walked round, it was quiet and calm ... when I went to pick him up, he was asleep in a rocking chair thing and he never falls asleep in those and they just left him – now if that had been me I would never have left him all hunched over even if it took him time to get back to sleep, I would have made sure he was more comfortable and then he was dead poorly when he came back ... and I cried myself to sleep that night. So the next day I went to this nursery. (Mother of Tim)

The second day nursery

The second nursery was also privately owned, and based in the city. It had no access to an outdoor area. To address this, children were taken on trips to the shops to buy the snack, and taken to the local park; the older children were taken on local transport to various locations. This lack of outdoor access was always a concern, because although the setting tried to address it through various means the children had very little regular access to a large area where they could experience space and freedom, which Margaret McMillan saw as their right. Margaret McMillan and her sister Rachel established nurseries which were a forerunner of the present agenda for giving more choice and opportunity for parents to be involved in their child's education. Within the nurseries, there was a great emphasis on nourishment, hygiene, exercise and fresh air and Margaret's methods still influence nurseries in England today.

As soon as he can toddle we introduce the child to a new environment, which is nevertheless his long lost natural home, his God-designed habitat, where his sense and spirit may be allowed to waken, and his impulse and activity will not meet unnatural obstacle or definite arrest. He is to live in the open air from the first, having shelter from rain, cold, and heat, every extreme and undue rigour of climate, but free to look upon the sky. (McMillan, 1930, p. 1)

This second nursery was also managed by one of the owners and was opened in 1995. There were 37 children aged from birth to 5 attending this nursery. The nursery was based in one room, with a small designated area for babies under 2. When parents were asked why they had chosen this nursery, two of them responded by saying:

It helped me. I often work until 6.00 pm, and I looked at the local ones and I would have been struggling if there had been an accident or something. I know they don't dump your child, but I didn't want to be late every night. My job gives me free parking opposite the nursery and that is how I saw it. (Mother of Georgina)

It is very near to work, so that if I had to because there was an emergency I can run round in 5 minutes. It is that accessibility as well. (Mother of Melanie)

This nursery is no longer registered with the same provider to offer day care for children.

The links between this second nursery and the findings of the study of Sam will be looked at in detail in Chapter 4.

The children

The following table lists the children involved in the study. Those children whose names are in bold are those whom I used in my final research for my PhD.

As many mothers now take extended maternity leave, the children observed in the day nurseries were often over 9 months of age when they first attended. This meant that the case studies did not really look at young babies, something that I was particularly interested in, and so the study of Sam, whom I started to observe when he was 8 days old, added another dimension to the case studies used within this book.

The settings that were used in the research, and those which will be referred to in general, are all nurseries that have achieved a 'good'

Name of child	Date of birth	Date observations started	Number of observations	Parent interviewed	Reasons for ceasing observations
Amy	March 03	19/2/04	15	Yes	Moved house
Mark	November 01	17/2/04	11	Yes	Observations stopped when 3
Ben	November 02	27/2/04	14	Yes	Observations stopped when 3
James	December 02	18/2/04	16	Yes	Observations stopped when 3
Harriet	October 01	27/2/04	3	Yes	Left to go to Independent School nursery
Felicity	August 01	17/2/04	7	No	Moved to maintained nursery school September 2004
Maisie	June 02	19/2/04	10	Yes	Observations stopped when 3
Josh	January 02	18/2/04	5	Yes	Left to go to funded playgroup September 2004
Tim	May 03	15/9/04	14	Yes	Observations stopped when 3
Lynda	October 03	14/12/04	15	No	Observations stopped when 3
Dan	April 04	15/12/04	5	Yes	Observations stopped when pattern of attendance changed
Martin	July 05	9/2/05	13	Yes	Moved house
Melanie	March 04	9/3/05	16	Yes	Observations stopped when 3
Georgina	January 04	9/2/05	16	Yes	Observations stopped when 3
Sam	August 04	20/8/04	31	Yes	Observations stopped when 3

Figure 1.1 The children involved in the case studies

or better outcome from their Ofsted inspections. All the settings described illustrate what good day care can look like in a range of different ways. A setting may not demonstrate good quality because of its lack of outdoor provision, but may demonstrate it through the way in which it supports young children's emotional wellbeing. It's important to remember that these are real settings battling with common constraints and problems, and that their successes and difficulties offer us an opportunity to reflect on how to deliver good quality care for babies and young children. Also, I think it is important to continue to challenge settings and practitioners, once they have started on the road to reflection and quality.

The baby cared for at home

Sam, the baby cared for at home by his mother, was the youngest of three children, as the older two children had already accessed out-of-home care, childminders, day nurseries and pre-school, whilst their mother returned to work for three days a week. Observing a baby at home as part of my research proved invaluable when looking at what out-of-home care can offer as a balance to a child staying at home with his mother. Staying at home to care for a child is in line with the thinking of Bowlby, but in today's economic climate it is not an option available to all families.

 Questions for reflection

- Consider how in your practice you embed the Vygotskian theory of the zone of proximal development. How do you challenge babies and young children through your interaction and support?
- Reflect on the different early years strategies for the countries of the UK. How could they contribute to your philosophy and practice?

Further reading

Gerhardt, S. (2010) *The Selfish Society.* London: Simon & Schuster UK Ltd.
This is a critical look at how society has focused more on economics to the detriment of children.

Dex, S. and Joshi, H. (2005) *Children of the 21st Century: From Birth to Nine Months.* Bristol: The Policy Press.

Hansen, K., Joshi, H. and Dex, S. (2010) *Children of the 21st Century: First Five Years v. 2* (UK Millennium Cohort Study Series). Bristol: The Policy Press.
The above two books document the outcomes so far of almost 19,000 children who were born at the beginning of the 21st century and give an insight into the policies that have impacted and are impacting on today's children.

The Scottish Government (2010) *Pre-Birth to Three: Positive Outcomes for Scotland's Children and Families*. Available at: www.ltscotland.org.uk/earlyyears/prebirthto three/nationalguidance/index.asp
This website gives the opportunity to look at all aspects of the innovative Scottish Framework for Early Years.

McMillan, M. (1930) *The Nursery School* (revised edition): London: J.M. Dent & Sons E.P. Dutton. Can be viewed on the following website: http://studentzone.roehampton.ac.uk/library/digital-collection/froebel-archive/nursery-school/index.html
The book details how Margaret and Rachel McMillan established their open-air nursery schools in Deptford, London. It gives an insight into the thinking and philosophy of the sisters and gives the reader the opportunity to question their own practice and reflect on the history of childcare and education in this country.

References

Ainsworth, M. (1969) Object Relations, Dependency, and Attachment: A Theoretical Review of the Infant–Mother Relationship. *Child Development,* 40(4): 969–1025.

Aistear (2010) *The Early Childhood Curriculum Framework*. Available at: www.ncca.ie/en/Curriculum_and_Assessment/Early_Childhood_and_ Primary_Education/Early_Childhood_Education/Framework–for_ Early_Learning/

Allen, G. (2011) *Early Intervention: The Next Steps*. Available at: http:// preventionaction.org/sites/all/files/Early%20intervention%20report. pdf

Bowlby, J. (1989) *The Making and Breaking of Affectional Bonds*. Oxon: Routledge.

Burman, E. (1994) *Deconstructing Developmental Psychology*. New York: Routledge.

David, T., Goouch, K., Powell, S. and Abbott, L. (2003) *Birth to Three Matters: A Review of the Literature*. Nottingham: DfES Publications.

DfES (2002) *Birth to Three Matters*. Nottingham: DfES Publications.

DfES (2007) *Statutory Framework for the Early Years Foundation Stage: Setting the Standards for Learning, Development and Care for Children from Birth to Five*. Nottingham: DfES.

Field, F. (2010) *The Foundation Years: Preventing Poor Children Becoming Poor Adults.* London: Cabinet Office.

Gopnik, A., Meltzoff, A. and Kuhl, P. (2001) *How Babies Think.* London: Phoenix.

HM Government (2011) *Opening Doors, Breaking Barriers: A Strategy for Social Mobility.* London: Cabinet Office.

James, A., Jenks, C. and Prout, A. (1998) *Theorising Childhood.* Cambridge: Polity Press.

McMillan, M. (1930) *The Nursery School (Revised edition).* London: J.M. Dent & Sons: E.P. Dutton.

Piaget, J. (1959) *Language and Thought of the Child.* London: Routledge & Kegan Paul Ltd.

The Scottish Government (2010) *Pre-Birth to Three: Positive Outcome for Scotland's Children and Families.* Edinburgh: Scottish Government.

Tickell, C. (2011) *The Early Years: Foundations for Life, Health and Learning. An Independent Report on the Early Years Foundation Stage to Her Majesty's Government.* London: DfE. Available at www.education.gov.uk/tickellreview

Vygotsky, L. (1978) *Mind in Society: The Development of Higher Psychological Processes.* London: Harvard University Press.

Vygotsky, L. (1986) *Thought and Language* (revised & edited by A. Kozulin, A.). London: The MIT Press.

Useful websites

www.education.gov.uk/childrenandyoungpeople/earlylearningand childcare

www.ncca.ie/en/Curriculum_and_Assessment/Early_Childhood_and_ Primary_Education/Early_Childhood_Education/Aistear_Toolkit

http://wales.gov.uk/topics/educationandskills/earlyyearshome/foundation_ phase/?lang=en

www.ltscotland.org.uk/earlyyears/prebirthtothree/index.asp

www.deni.gov.uk/index/pre-school-education-pg.htm

2 The Emotional Environment

This chapter will:

- look at the emotional environment as an important factor in the development of babies and young children
- discuss companionable learning
- consider the importance of Attachment Theory
- discuss the importance of interaction in babies and young children's emotional wellbeing
- stress the importance of creating emotionally safe environments
- look at the Leuven Scales of Wellbeing and Involvement.

Great emphasis is placed on children learning to read and write as the precursor to all learning but unless a baby and young child feel emotionally secure and safe, no learning will take place. We only have to look at our reactions as adults to know that when we are stressed, nervous or emotionally uncomfortable, we do not operate at the same level as when we are happy, content and have a feeling of wellbeing. This is reminiscent of Goleman's (1996) work on multiple intelligences where he highlights the link between emotional intelligence and future success. He asserts that traditional IQ scores are not always indicators of success, but that we need emotional competencies to understand how to use our skills, such as intellect.

The Labour government of 1997 to 2010 in the UK highlighted the personal, social and emotional development of babies and young children through its political agenda for the early years, which began with the *National Childcare Strategy* (DfEE, 1998) with the aim '… to ensure good quality, affordable childcare for children aged 0–14 in every neighbourhood, including both formal childcare and support for informal arrangements', as part of their Sure Start agenda. This was subsequently followed by the *Every Child Matters* programme (HM Government, 2003) which headlined the following outcomes for children and against which all settings in England are, at the time of writing, still inspected by Ofsted today:

- Be healthy.
- Stay safe.
- Enjoy and achieve.
- Make a positive contribution.
- Achieve economic wellbeing.

As one of their initiatives to achieve these outcomes for children, the government established a training package, *Social and Emotional Aspects of Development* (SEAD) (DCSF, 2008), to develop practitioner knowledge in this area of child development. For many local authorities, this has become one of their key core training initiatives, in the belief that if settings can get this right for the babies and children in their care, then both emotional and cognitive learning can take place.

Research has told us much about the way in which babies' psychological development has an impact on their future learning and how they engage with society as they grow up (Fonagy, 2001; Hobson, 2002; Roberts, 2010; Allen, 2011). It is therefore important that when looking at the environments of babies and young children, we first look at their emotional environment, as this is the one which will have the greatest impact on their future learning and development. As Gerhardt (2004, p. 196) writes, 'Babyhood is an intense, concentrated moment of development that can have a disproportionate impact on our lives ...'.

In her later book *The Selfish Society* (Gerhardt, 2010), she examines the way in which the wider society and the political perspectives of a time can have an impact on the emotional development of babies, which in turn has an impact on their emotional strength when they are adults. She states that '"Childcare" is a word which conveys physical and educational care, not a powerful relationship which carries so much human and spiritual meaning' (p. 201). Her concerns are that society is forcing many parents to make the decision to put their child into care for economic reasons, and as a result of this babies and young children are being 'forced' to have emotional experiences before they are developmentally ready to do so: 'The drive for everyone to be *economically* self-sufficient has pushed us into an expectation that everyone should be *emotionally* self-sufficient – even babies' (2010, p. 203). In view of this change in society, it is all the more important to get the emotional environment right for those children in childcare.

Roberts (2010) suggests a theory of wellbeing, 'companionable learning', which is closely linked to the theory of sustained shared thinking (Sylva et al., 2003) and Vygotsky's theory of the zone of proximal development (1978). Roberts (2010) identifies five companionable learning principles:

1 Companionable attention – those things that a baby or young child needs.
2 Agency in companionable play – play where children develop a sense of self and their position in relation to others.
3 Anchored children – all those times where the physical presence of the companion is a necessity.
4 Companionable apprenticeship – those episodes of play when children are involved in 'real life'.
5 Children's personal time and space – those times when, just like adults, babies need space for themselves, to be on their own.

These principles support children's wellbeing from birth and are a way in which practitioners could develop a framework to support the babies and young children in their care.

The Australian Government's early years learning framework *Belonging, Being and Becoming* (2009) stresses the importance to children of wellbeing. It sees this as the thread that draws the child's learning together: 'Without a strong sense of wellbeing it is difficult to have a sense of *belonging* to trust others and feel confident in *being,* and to optimistically engage in experiences that contribute to *becoming.*'

Out-of-home environments for babies and children under 2 can be very stressful, when they have not had the opportunities to manage and self-regulate their emotions. As practitioners are *in loco parentis*, it is important for them to be able to support babies and young children in being able to manage their own emotions. *The Effective Provision of Pre-school Education* (EPPE) research (Sylva et al., 2003) found that attendance in day care prior to 2 years of age can lead to some slight behaviour problems for a small group of children. It was found that these issues were reduced depending on the quality of the pre-school provision.

Another longitudinal study which is being carried out in the USA (2001) is the National Institute of Child Health and Human Development (NICHD) *Study of Early Child Care and Youth Development* which began in 1989 to look at the relationship between children's care experiences and children's developmental outcomes. The results from Phase 1 show that the average age at which children in the study started in non-maternal care was just over 3 months and that by 12 months over 68.6% were accessing regular non-maternal care. The study concludes, as did the

Project (1997–2004), that smaller groups, lower child-to-adult ratios, less authoritarian child-rearing beliefs and a safe, clean and stimulating environment impact on the quality of care received. This quality of care is closely linked to social and emotional development.

Attachment

The time spent in care is also found to be a factor in mother–child attachment. This attachment is the bonding that usually occurs between mother and baby at birth. This bonding or attachment is not always a given as Leach (2010) identifies when she discusses the problems of some mothers in forming an appropriate attachment with their young child, usually as a consequence of post-natal depression. Although the bond between mother and baby is seen as the strongest, babies can form multiple attachments, often when they attend out-of-home care settings, as well as with members of their extended family. It is therefore the bond between mother and baby which is the strongest and the one most affected by babies spending extended hours in care settings. Bowlby's attachment theory was based on society's belief that a mother's role is to remain at home with young children (Bowlby, 1989, p. 17): ' … separation from "his" mother after "he" has formed an emotional relationship with her can be so damaging to the development of "his" personality.'

Bowlby's theory was taken up after the Second World War to dissuade women from working, after they had provided an important role in sustaining the economy by working during the war. After the disruption of the war years, this theory appealed to many in society and was interpreted as a call for mothers to stay at home (Penn, 2005). The ending of the war meant that women were no longer needed to fulfill the role of men in the workplace, and so Bowlby's theory was used as an emotional weapon to encourage mothers to stay at home to look after their young children, although Bowlby insisted 'No such views have been expressed by me' (1969, p. 303).

In his work, Rutter (1972) refuted Bowlby's attachment theory by asserting that motherhood/attachment is not an innate quality, and that for some children being in the care of their mother was a detriment rather than an advantage. In his work, Rutter looked at the multiple attachments that children can form and concluded that provided the quality of care outside the home was good then children would not suffer. As Nutbrown and Page (2008, p. 24) affirm: 'Indeed, some may argue that a lack of multiple attachments in the early part of life could also be detrimental to babies' social development.'

The work of Bowlby was furthered by Ainsworth (1969) who looked at separation anxiety. This involved putting children in strange situations and observing their differing patterns of behaviour when the mother was in, out of and returning to the room and also by introducing a stranger. The differing reactions of the child indicated whether a child was secure or not. Burman (1994) and Bruer (1999) rightly questioned the validity and ethics of the strange situation arguing that it is wrong to suggest that children of working mothers are distressed by being left in care, raising the point that for these children care is seen as part of their everyday life and that attachment theory negates the close relationships and bonds that children have with other carers apart from their parents.

The NICHD (2001) research has looked at how the emotional wellbeing of babies and young children is affected by periods of separation:

> ... analyses of attachment at 15 months showed that children who spent more hours in child care *and* had mothers who were relatively insensitive and unresponsive were at heightened risk for insecure infant–mother attachments. At 24 months, spending more hours in care was associated with mothers' reports of lower social competence and caregivers' reports of more problem behaviours. (NICHD, 2001, p. 485)

Of interest in the NICHD Phase 1 is the conclusion that it is the mother–child relationship that has the greater impact on a child's development, both cognitive and social, no matter how much non-maternal care is accessed. It is the impact of external effects, divorce, changes in care arrangements, family relocation and, on a larger scale, the history of the time within the family that appear to have the greatest influence on development. The history of time can be the political and economic factor which influences a child's upbringing; for example, in a time of recession carers may become unemployed, or the society/culture where a baby is bought up may be affected by strikes, such as in the mining communities of the 1970s and 1980s. It is these factors which can be found reflected in Bronfenbrenner's (1979) ecological model of development.

Bronfenbrenner (1979) believed that to understand interactions, it was necessary not only to be aware of how others influence children's development within these interactions, but also how children influence their own development by the way in which they initiate interaction and how they influence their environments. Bronfenbrenner describes the ecological environment as '... a set of nested structures, each inside the next, like a set of Russian dolls. At the innermost level is the immediate setting containing the developing person. This can be the home, the classroom …' (Bronfenbrenner, 1979, p. 3). He also stated that the wider environment could have an impact on the development of children so that a change to the economy of the society in which the child lives could have either a positive or negative impact on the future development of that child. The impact of the economy on young children is of importance at the beginning of the 21st century because of the world economic crisis.

This emphasis of the impact of the wider environment on a child's development is particularly relevant to the children observed for the case studies within my research. Bronfenbrenner (1979, p. 165) recognized that there was a lack of research into the impact that day care can have on children's development and he suggested that:

> … the impact of day care and preschool on the nation's families and on the society at large may have a more profound consequence than any direct effects for the development of human beings in modern industrialized societies.

The NICHD (2001) research in the USA and the EPPE (Sylva et al., 2003) and FCCC (Leach et al., 2006a and b) in the UK, are in line with Bronfenbrenner's theory that research on children's development should be longitudinal. The results to date of these studies are recognizing that there are factors outside of the setting and the numbers of hours attended that are influencing children's development. These studies, as discussed previously, highlight the importance of the home environment and the quality of the childcare received. The influences of the family can impact on a child's development, even if they are attending a high quality childcare setting.

Historically, theorists have observed children with the aim of obtaining a scientific conclusion so they have not needed to refer to the outside factors that influence child development.

When looking at this issue, Bronfenbrenner (1979, p. 205) raised the following as one of his hypotheses:

> The developmental potential of a day care or preschool setting depends on the extent to which supervising adults create and maintain opportunities for the involvement of children in a variety of progressively more complex molar activities and interpersonal structures that are commensurate with the child's evolving capacities and allow her sufficient balance of power to introduce innovations of her own.

When babies and young children are accessing care out of the home, the amount of interest that providers show in gathering evidence about the different systems that can have an effect on a child, as illustrated by Bronfenbrenner's ecological theory where the child is at the centre with all the external influences surrounding her, is questionable. It is then all of these concentric circles which impact on a baby's development. This evidence gathered from home is vital, if the baby is to feel emotionally safe and secure in the nursery environment.

Sharing information

When practitioners gather information from parents, it mainly centres on the child's routines and their care needs. Although these are important factors, this could be extended to asking about the child's position in the family (and paying attention to this detail as highlighted in Chapter 4), the names of all those adults and children who play an important part in that child's life (siblings, grandparents, aunts, family friends) and where they live and how this affects their everyday lives. Figure 2.1 illustrates the way in which Bronfenbrenner's model could be used to gain a wider knowledge of many of the factors influencing a child. At first glance, many would say this was intrusive but with this deeper knowledge of a child, a setting would be better able to provide an environment which could make the child feel safe and secure and so have an impact on his emotional wellbeing.

Child's name	
Mother's name	
Father's name	
Brother's name	
Sister's name	
Where has s/he been cared for?	
Where does s/he live?	
Schools/Pre-schools/Other settings	
Religious/cultural influences	
Grandparents	
Pets	
Work	
Leisure	
Local area/government	

Figure 2.1   A model for gathering information about a child's whole story

If a model such as this was used, practitioners would know more about children's early experiences. For example, by knowing about a child's access or lack of access to a garden at home, for instance if they lived in a flat, then practitioners could plan experiences for that particular child which would involve access to the outside.

Another way in which a setting could ensure that babies and children feel safe and secure within their environment is illustrated in the following case study from one of the day nurseries where the two worlds of the child, nursery and home, are bridged.

 Case study 2

When parents visit the nursery to register their child, they are given a disposable camera when they leave. The manager asks them to take photographs, using half of the film, of the people/things that are important in their child's life. This can be photographs of the child's immediate and extended family, favourite toys, books and other objects, their bedroom, different rooms in the house, etc. On one occasion, the manager told me that one mother had taken a photograph of the sky, and when questioned as to why she had chosen to take this picture, she replied that this was what her baby saw when she was put outside to sleep in the garden. The rest of the film is then used by the setting to take photographs of the baby/child during their first week. These photographs are then used to make a special book for the child, which is kept within reach and which is added to as the child progresses through the nursery. On many occasions when I have visited, a child has gone to get *their* book to tell me all about themselves and the history of their lives and their time in the nursery.

This case study shows how a setting can use information about a child to create an emotionally safe and secure place for them.

The following is another technique which can be used to bridge the gap between home and nursery, which has been effective when children begin to attend a mainstream setting and which could also be used as babies and young children begin to attend an out-of-home setting. When a baby or young child is registered to attend a setting, they and their parents are usually assigned a key person with whom they can develop a close relationship. The key person could write a letter to the family, introducing herself and telling them something (only that which she is willing to share) about herself. A photograph could also be enclosed to again create a sense of familiarity. This way of introducing the key person, both verbally and pictorially, goes some way to breaking down the barriers of unfamiliarity and is a path to forging a deeper relationship.

Wellbeing

As adults, we frequently talk about what body language and facial expression tell us about family, friends, colleagues and acquaintances. We know that when we are happy and interested in something, we become motivated and we achieve so much more in our daily home and working lives. This is the same for children, so it is imperative that we strive to make their environments ones where this can occur. In order to ascertain whether or not we have been successful, the work that has been done on experiential learning by Ferre Laevers (Laevers et al.,1997) in Leuven gives us one possible model by which to measure babies' and young children's levels of wellbeing and involvement. Laevers describes wellbeing in the following manner:

> Children with a high level of well-being feel great. They enjoy life to the full. They have fun, take joy in each other and in their surroundings. They radiate vitality as well as relaxation and inner peace. They adopt an open and receptive attitude towards their environment. They are spontaneous and can fully be themselves. Well-being is linked to self-confidence, a good degree of self-esteem and resilience. All this is based on being in touch with themselves, with their own feelings and experiences, fresh and pure. (Laevers et al.,1997, p. 8)

This description can clearly be seen to link to the Personal, Social and Emotional (PSE) development of children which is why its use as an assessment tool is particularly valuable. Practitioners can use this tool as part of their ongoing observations to evaluate and reflect on how the children are responding to their environments, and then use this reflection to adapt what is on offer to meet the needs of individual children. The use of this tool with children under 3 years of age is of value as their PSE development is one of the core features of their development, along with Communication and Physical Development.

In Laevers' work, babies and children are observed and then assessed according to the Leuven scales of wellbeing and involvement. Laevers (1994) describes wellbeing as: '... show[ing] us how much the educational environment succeeds in helping the child to feel at home, to be her/himself, to remain in contact with her/himself and have her/his emotional needs (the need for attention, recognition, competence ...) fulfilled'; and involvement as: ' ... a special state characterized by concentration, intense experience, intrinsic motivation, a flow of energy and a high level of satisfaction connected with the fulfillment of the exploratory drive.' The scales are a five-point rating, where level 1 for involvement describes no activity; and where level 5 describes sustained intense activity; and where level 1 for wellbeing describes levels of discomfort and where level 5 is evidenced by clear physical and facial signs of happiness and enjoyment.

The scales that Laevers has developed show that when a child is involved in his play, there is a deeper level of emotional wellbeing which in turn enhances a child's development. During the observations of Sam, who was cared for at home by his mother, he was introduced to a treasure basket and, during this first treasure basket observation, the Leuven Involvement Scale as adapted for young children by Forbes (2004, pp. 82–3), which she uses to identify a baby's involvement in their treasure basket play, was used to assess his levels of wellbeing and involvement.

 Case study 3: Sam at 7 months old

Sam studies the basket and there is a change in his activity. His breathing and his arm movements are much more defined. He doesn't like the touch of the loofah fish – the touch puts him off.

He reaches into the basket and begins to engage with a wide range of the resources – the scarf, the spoons which he returns to again and again, the shells and the brushes. He holds them up and really explores and investigates them. He is absorbed and is rarely distracted other than when he hits himself on the head – this resource is removed. Rachel comments on the pace with which he is touching the things in the basket.

When looking at the child involvement signals, Sam is concentrating and there is a definite increase in the effort that he is putting into this play. Sam is definitely persisting in this play – he sustains the play for 20 minutes with few episodes of distraction; for example, he bumps himself and then is quickly reassured and soon returns to his play. He is definitely satisfied with the play.

After this initial observation, Rachel, Sam's mother, was asked to continue to use the Involvement Scales when Sam was playing with the treasure basket. Figure 2.2 shows the notes that she made.

Anyone working with babies and young children should be encouraged to use the Leuven scales to establish the children's emotional wellbeing and involvement whenever they observe babies and young children in their play and also when they are engaged in

Date	Length of play	Levels – Involvement Scales
28/3/05	10 minutes	Level 4: 8 minutes reducing to levels 3/2 at the end
30/3/05	15 minutes	Level 4/5: 10 minutes
		Level 3/2: 5 minutes – wanted bottle
2/4/05	10 minutes	Level 4/5: 8 minutes
		Level 3: 1 minute
		Level 2: 1 minute
4/4/05	5 minutes	Level 4
9/4/05	10 minutes	Level 4: 7 minutes
		Level 3: 2 minutes
		Level 1: 1 minute
13/4/05	12 minutes	Level 4/5: 8 minutes
		Level 3: 4 minutes
17/4/05	6 minutes	Level 4: 5 minutes
		Level 3: 1 minute
19/4/05	10 minutes	Level 4/5: 7 minutes
		Level 3: 3 minutes
24/4/05	9 minutes	Level 4: 4 minutes
		Level 3: 4 minutes
		Level 2: 1 minute
28/4/05	10 minutes	Level 5: 5 minutes
		Level 4: 2 minutes
		Level 3: 3 minutes
1/5/05	5 minutes	Level 3: 4 minutes
		Level 2: 1 minute – needed a sleep

Levels of involvement were affected by the following:

• Familiarity
• Presence of siblings
• Physical state – feed/sleep

Figure 2.2   A timetable of Sam's involvement with the treasure basket

social interactions. When Rachel used the scales to observe Sam's play with the treasure basket, she decided to introduce Sam to his other toys as she did with the treasure basket and also to rotate them to break the familiarity cycle. Rachel liked the basket because Sam was able to use the resources differently in different combinations on different occasions. These observations made by a mother show the value of observing babies and young children to plan for their learning, and also to ensure that their emotional as well as their cognitive needs are being met; these two are interdependent, on one another.

Interaction

The emotional expressions of caregivers help children lay the foundations of their emotional development. This development begins in the early years and mainly occurs within family relationships. In research into the brain development of newborn babies (Gopnik et al., 1999), it was seen that babies reacted positively to voices and facial expressions. Murray and Andrews (2000, p. 19) also carried out close studies of babies from birth to look at the development of their communication:

> One of the dramatic abilities of the newborn that shows she is ready for social contact with other people is her ability to imitate another person's facial expression

and by 9 months,

> ... they can tell the difference between expressions of happiness and sadness and anger, and even can recognize that a happy-looking face, a face with a smile and crinkly eyes, goes with the chirp of a happy tone of voice. (Gopnik et al., 1999, p. 28)

Trevarthen has shown in his research that the use of 'motherese' or Infant Directed Speech (IDS) and nursery rhymes can affect the emotional responses of young babies; babies are more emotionally responsive to this type of speech. Trevarthen talks about the '... sensitive two-way mirroring of the enhanced emotional values of expression that overrides the great difference in maturity of the baby and the adult' (Trevarthen and Malloch, 2002, p. 12). This mother–child musical partnership is not always present. When a mother does not react vocally and facially to her baby, then the baby can become distressed and withdrawn. When mothers have been videoed, the response of the baby is apparent; when the mother uses her voice and facial expression in response to her baby, s/he becomes animated, physically and vocally, whereas if the mother adopts 'a still face' (in an experiment pioneered by Lynn Murray), the baby becomes withdrawn, showing no physical or facial responses, and within seconds can become very distressed. Trevarthen's theory of mother and baby in partnership is an example of the Vygotskian concept of the zone of proximal development (ZPD) where the mother is scaffolding the baby's developing social, communication and emotional skills. Vygotsky (1978) describes ZPD as the distance between the actual developmental level as determined by independent problem solving and the level of potential development as determined through problem solving under adult guidance or in collaboration with more capable peers.

In a nursery setting, this means establishing a relationship between the adult and the baby. The following case study is of a 1-year-old baby. In this case study, the adult moderates the tone of her voice in response to the conversations that she is having with Melanie. Of merit is the way in which Melanie is offered choices – things aren't just 'done' to her – she is only lifted out when she has indicated that this is what she wants. It is the attention of the adult, which Melanie craves, that ensures she is emotionally safe and secure.

 Case study 4: Melanie at 1 year old

When I arrive at the nursery, Melanie is in a bouncing chair alongside an adult.

- The adult is gently bouncing the chair. She is talking very gently to Melanie – she is soothing her and Melanie is turning her attention towards the adult.
- Melanie is holding up her arms and playing with the sleeves of her top. She is also holding her hands in front of her face and looking at them very closely. She repeats these actions several times.
- The adult then faces the bouncing chair to the mirror hanging on the fence so that Melanie can see herself.
- Melanie notices that she is not quite as close to the adult so she makes this known and the adult pulls her in closer and moves the mirror. Again, when she is close, the adult talks to her in gentle, soothing tones.
- Melanie now takes to bouncing herself in the chair – she is obviously enjoying this and puts all of her energies into making the chair bounce.
- Melanie is obviously teething and occasionally she turns to the adult for reassurance, which she gets. The adult tells her that it will soon be better.
- This works and Melanie resumes her bouncing, now clapping at the same time.
- When she looks at the adult, she talks to her and then she continues bouncing.
- The adult then asks Melanie if she would like to get out of the chair – she is given the choice and Melanie answers by resuming her bouncing. She pulls herself to turn around and then she talks to herself in the mirror.
- She is babbling and talking, she is very happy and content.
- Melanie now makes it known that she wants to get out of the chair so the adult lifts her out.
- Melanie now crawls off in the room.

In a home setting, the relationship between mother and child is usually more secure, and as a consequence bonding is not normally an issue. In one of the case studies, Sam was observed at home with his mother for three years. The greatest influencing factor on Sam's development was the involvement of a skilled and knowledgeable adult, his mother. The initial observations reveal a strong bond between mother and son. This bond not only manifested itself in the love and care that Rachel gave to her son but the quality of the communication and interaction. At an early stage, Rachel is able to interpret Sam's cries and is also skilled in the use of 'motherese' (Trevarthen and Malloch, 2002).

> Yes there is definitely one of those, a bit fed up, not really sure and those ones we're trying to leave a bit longer with because sometimes he will just give up with it. It sounds like a cry but a lot more spaced out in between and a lot weaker, there's not really that much effort in it. Whereas when he gets angry he will be covered in sweat, his hair will be soaking wet – when he definitely wants something, there's a real difference between it. (Rachel, Sam's mother)

The following observation supports the manner in which Rachel talks and responds to Sam and how her knowledge of his likes and dislikes impacts on his emotional security:

> When Rachel puts Sam down on his mat he becomes instantly agitated but once he makes eye contact with his mother he immediately quietens, this calmness intensifies as Rachel holds his hands by his side. This is a favourite interaction and links in with the fact that Sam still likes to be swaddled when asleep. Sam begins to get agitated but again the instant Rachel begins to interact with him he settles. Rachel uses gentle tones and directs her speech to him as she makes eye contact. Sam responds by moving his mouth in reply; this is definitely a conversation.

Whenever Rachel was with Sam she engaged in talk with him; making good eye contact, leaving spaces for him to respond, respecting him by telling him what she was doing and interpreting his responses. Observing these interactions and seeing the way in which Sam's language and social skills developed with skill and confidence, highlighted the need for adults in day care settings to engage with this type of practice and to establish good partnerships with parents so that parents can pass on the knowledge that they have about their children. The importance of this type of interaction is echoed in the words of Gopnik et al. (1999, p. 28) that I also referred to earlier in this chapter:

> ... they can tell the difference between expressions of happiness and sadness and anger, and even can recognize that a happy-looking face, a face with a smile and crinkly eyes, goes with the chirp of a happy tone of voice.

In the days of modern technology where people can interact via electronic devices, it is even more important for parents and practitioners to engage their children in direct human conversation. I may be getting old when I shudder upon seeing young mothers pushing their prams with their iPods or their mobile phones to their ears. I am not a Luddite and I have a mobile phone and I love listening to my iPod when I am walking along, but I am not pushing a pram with a baby eager to absorb all the interaction possible.

In contrast, some prospective parents might spend hours researching for the best pram. One young couple, who were aware of all the work conducted by the National Literacy Trust on the Talk to Your Baby website (www.talktoyourbaby.com), found it really hard to choose the right pram for their new baby. The research shows that, '... the unsociable design of children's buggies is a factor contributing to the poor language and communication skills of many children starting nursery or school. Young children need face-to-face communication to fully develop as sociable talkers and learners'. This campaign has been further enhanced by the 10-minute video produced by Norland College showing what it feels like to be a baby in a forward-facing buggy; it is really quite a scary experience (see www.literacytrust.org.uk/resources/videos/1859_norland_college_forward-facing_buggy_ride). All of this demonstrates the importance of interaction, not only for children's language development but also for their emotional wellbeing.

As they develop, infants interpret positive and negative facial and vocal expressions, which Mumme et al. (1996) call 'social referencing'; if a negative expression is shown to a particular toy the child will then avoid it. Alongside early emotional development is the establishing of secure relationships. The most important of these is that between parent and child:

> In general, a secure parent–child attachment relationship is associated with enhanced emotion understanding, greater cooperation, less negativity and decreased aggression in close relationships, as well as other indications of positive emotional growth in early childhood. (Thompson and Lagattuta, 2006, p. 324)

This establishment of secure relationships links back to Roberts' (2010) five companionable learning principles, discussed earlier.

The cross-political party research by Graham Allen MP and the Rt Hon. Iain Duncan-Smith MP (2008) looks deeper into the question of the link between good parenting and the impact that this can have on 'build[ing] the human foundations of a healthy, functioning society'. In their report, they discuss breaking the generational dysfunctioning of families by having a 0–18 early intervention process where not only is emphasis placed on the 0–3 age range but it also focuses on young adults in secondary schools, giving them the knowledge of what it is to become a good parent and how as a parent they can support their children's learning and so end the dysfunctional society that has been the topic of much debate over recent years. Something which is often neglected by politicians is the need to keep initiatives longitudinal because '... a generational problem will take a generation to fix'. This need for a long-term perspective of changing outcomes for children is reflected in the Scottish Early Years Framework (The Scottish Government, 2008), in which they state: 'Early years investment is not a magic bullet ... it will take a concerted and long term effort across a range of policies and services to achieve a transformation in outcomes.'

Allen and Duncan-Smith (2008) recognize that in the UK we spend too much time focusing on educational attainment, whereas the models from countries such as Sweden and Finland are about not introducing young children to formal schooling until they are 8 or 9 years of age, and yet still they are at the top of education attainment leagues. They put this down to the fact that ' ... the first few years of school life have been spent building the social and emotional abilities which make children "school ready".' As parents, we may all talk of wanting our children to be happy and yet many may still feel that the only way that this can be achieved is through academic success. Perhaps if we left our children to become emotionally secure before introducing an academic curriculum, then fewer of our children would become disaffected as they progress though our current target-led education system. In Wales, the Foundation Phase (WAG, 2008) is for children aged 3–7 and has at its core Personal and Social Development, Well-Being and Cultural Diversity, reflecting all those elements discussed in this chapter as being crucial for the basis of future learning.

 Questions for reflection

Think about your own practice and that of others in your setting in relation to the centrality of babies and young children's emotional environment:

- What are the links between the home and the setting when babies first attend?
- How do you think you could effectively use the Leuven scales for wellbeing and involvement to reflect on your observations of children? For further information on the scales, see http://www.kindengezin.be/img/sics-ziko-manual.pdf

Further reading 📖

Gerhardt, S. (2004) *Why Love Matters: How Affection Shapes a Baby's Brain.* Hove: Brunner-Routledge.
This book is essential reading to gain an understanding of how emotions impact on the brain development of babies and young children.

Hansen, K., Joshi, H. and Dex, S. (eds) (2010) *Children of the 21st Century: The First Five Years.* Bristol: The Policy Press.
Based on the research findings of the first five years of the Millennium Cohort study, this book raises questions about the implications for policy and practice.

Palmer, S. (2006) *Toxic Childhood.* London: Orion Books.
This book discusses controversial questions around the problems that society is having in bringing up the next generation.

References

Ainsworth, M. (1969) Object Relations, Dependency, and Attachment: A Theoretical Review of the Infant–Mother Relationship. *Child Development,* 40(4): 969–1025.

Allen, G. (2011) *Early Intervention: The Next Steps.* Available at: http://preventionaction.org/sites/all/files/Early%20intervention%20report.pdf

Allen, G. and Duncan-Smith, I. (2008) *Early Intervention: Good Parents, Great Kids, Better Citizens.* Available at: www.centreforsocialjustice.org.uk/client/downloads/EarlyInterventionpaperFINAL.pdf

Bowlby, J. (1969) *Attachment and Loss: Vol. 1. Attachment.* New York: Basic Books.

Bowlby, J. (1989) *The Making and Breaking of Affectional Bonds.* Oxon: Routledge.

Bronfenbrenner, U. (1979) *The Ecology of Human Development: Experiments by Nature and Design.* London: Harvard University Press.

Bruer, J. (1999) *The Myth of the First Three Years.* New York: Free Press.

Burman, E. (1994) *Deconstructing Developmental Psychology.* New York: Routledge.

Department for Children, Schools and Families (DCSF) (2008) *Social and Emotional Aspects of Development.* Nottingham: DCSF.

Department for Education and Employment (DfEE) (1998) *Meeting the Childcare Challenge.* London: The Stationery Office.

Fonagy, P. (2001) *Attachment Theory and Psychoanalysis.* New York: Other Press.

Forbes, R. (2004) *Beginning to Play*. Maidenhead: Open University Press.

Gerhardt, S. (2004) *Why Love Matters: How Affection Shapes a Baby's Brain*. Hove: Brunner-Routledge.

Gerhardt, S. (2010) *The Selfish Society*. London: Simon & Schuster.

Goleman, D. (1996) *Emotional Intelligence*. London: Bloomsbury Publishing.

Gopnik, A., Meltzoff, A. and Kuhl, P. (1999) *How Babies Think*. London: Phoenix.

HM Government (2003) *Every Child Matters*. Department for Education and Skills. London: The Stationery Office.

Hobson, P. (2002) *The Cradle of Thought*. London: Macmillan.

Laevers, F. (1994) *The Innovative Project Experiential Education*. Leuven: Centre for Experiential Education.

Laevers, F., Vandenbussche, E., Kog, M. and Depondt, L. (1997) *A Process-oriented Child Monitoring System for Young Children*. Experiential Education Series No 2. Leuven: Centre for Experiential Education.

Leach, P. (2010) *The Essential First Year: What Babies Need Parents to Know*. London: Dorling Kindersley.

Leach, P., Barnes, J., Malmberg, L., Sylva, K., Stein, A. and the FCCC team (2006a) The Quality of Different Types of Child Care at 10 and 18 Months: A Comparison Between Types and Factors Related to Quality. *Early Child Development and Care*, 176(5): 553–73.

Leach, P., Barnes, J., Nichols, M., Goldin, J., Stein, A., Sylva, K., Malmberg, L. and the FCCC team (2006b) Childcare Before Six Months of Age: A Qualitative Study. *Infant and Child Development*, 15(5): 471–502.

Mumme, D., Fernald, A. and Herrera, C. (1996) Infants' Responses to Facial and Emotional Signals in a Social Referencing Paradigm. *Child Development*, 67 (6): 3219–37.

Murray, L. and Andrews, L. (2000) *The Social Baby*. Richmond: CP Publishing.

NICHD Early Child Care Research Network (2001) Nonmaternal Care and Family Factors in Early Development: An Overview of the NICHD Study of Early Child Care. *Applied Developmental Psychology*, 22: 457–92.

Nutbrown, C. and Page, J. (2008) *Working with Babies and Children from Birth to Three*. London: Sage.

Penn, H. (2005) *Understanding Early Childhood: Issues and Controversies*. Maidenhead: Open University Press.

Roberts, R. (2010) *Wellbeing from Birth*. London: Sage.

Rutter, M. (1972) *Maternal Deprivation Reassessed*. Harmondsworth: Penguin.

Sylva, K., Meluish, E., Sammons, P., Siraj-Blatchford, I., Taggart, B. and Elliot, K. (2003) *The Effective Provision of Pre-School Education (EPPE)*

Project: Findings from the Pre-School Period (Research Brief No: RBX15-03). London: DfES Publications.

The Australian Government (2009) *Belonging, Being and Becoming.* Available at: www.deewr.gov.au/Earlychildhood/Policy-Agenda/Quality/Documents/Final%20EYLA%20Report%20-%20Framework%20WEB.pdf

The Scottish Government (2008) *The Early Years Framework.* Edinburgh: Scottish Government.

Thompson, R. and Lagattuta, K. (2006) Feeling and Understanding: Early Emotional Development. In K. McCartney, K. and D. Phillips (eds), *Blackwell Handbook of Early Childhood Development.* Malden, MA: Blackwell Publishing.

Trevarthen, C. and Malloch, S. (2002) Musicality and Music Before Three: Human Vitality and Invention Shared with Pride. *Zero to Three,* September, 23(1): 10–18.

Vygotsky, L. (1978) *Mind in Society: The Development of Higher Psychological Processes.* London: Harvard University Press.

WAG (2008) *The Welsh Foundation Framework.* Cardiff: Welsh Assembly Government.

Useful websites

www.kindengezin.be/img/sics-ziko-manual.pdf

www.literacytrust.org.uk/resources/videos/1859_norland_college_forward-facing_buggy_ride

www.talktoyourbaby.org.uk

www.wales.gov.uk

www.earlychildhoodaustralia.org.au/resource_themes/eylf_early_years_learning_framework.html

3 The Role of Adults in the Environment

This chapter will:

- discuss the importance of attachment at separation
- demonstrate why the key person system is effective, and how it works
- discuss leadership and management's role within the key person system
- focus on the role of the adult in out-of-home care settings
- explain the importance of Continuing Professional Development.

We only have to look at brain research to understand why the adult is important to the development of babies and young children. From birth, babies are programmed to recognize the human face (Murray and Andrews, 2000) and research has shown that from the time she is just minutes old, a baby will imitate the facial expressions of a human. A baby is born with the need to learn, and the best way in which she can do this is through interaction with adults.

When looking at the early years practitioner, it is hard to define what qualities they should have. I have always struggled with those who say that love of children and patience is all that is needed. These are certainly qualities which one would expect to find, but the skill is finding the practitioner who not only enjoys being with children, but also has a sound understanding of how babies and children develop. It is with this depth of knowledge that the practitioner can understand what she is observing and assessing, and reflect on how she can move a child's development and understanding forwards. Another quality which is of crucial importance is an innovative approach to practice, that empowers children and babies to learn through their experiences. The best practitioners are those who follow the children's lead and who are genuinely involved. Young children are perceptive and know when an adult is 'faking' their enjoyment. A good early years practitioner is one who does not have to speak all of the time, and can sit and play alongside children in quiet reflection. All practitioners need these qualities, but they are of particular importance for those adults working with the youngest children. The baby room is the foundation of any nursery; it is here that the foundations for future learning and development are laid, so it is of vital importance that we place quality practitioners in this room, practitioners who see the potential of the babies in their care.

Attachment and separation

Since the launch of the National Childcare Strategy (DfEE, May 1998), there has been an increase in the number of out-of-home childcare providers, with babies and young children spending longer hours separated from their primary caregivers; in most cases this is parents. This separation, according to Bowlby (1989), Ainsworth (1969) and Belsky (2001, p. 846), has detrimental effects on the developing child:

> ... more than twenty hours per week of such care posed risks for the infant–parent relationships and for psychological and behavioural adjustment during the toddler, pre-school and early primary school years.

The following case study shows the bond that develops between mother and child. The case study starts when Sam is 8 days old, and concludes with an observation when Sam is 19 months old. The sequence of observations shows how the bond and attachment is formed between mother and child, and how this progresses to incorporating a wider group of familiar figures, his grandfather and myself. What is interesting is that, at 19 months, Sam shows distress when separated from his mother and his normal routine, emphasizing that babies and young children need the familiarity of carers and routine to maintain their equilibrium.

 Case study 5: Sam at 8 days old

When Rachel is talking to Sam, there is intensity in the way he follows her voice. I asked Rachel if she felt that he saw her? She said that he is focusing at what she called feeding distance; she also said that he was intense in his look. He still has the foetal curve and nestles into Rachel's body when she is holding him over her shoulder. Sam looks very contented and there is a peacefulness about him as he sleeps. One of the interesting comments that Rachel makes is how she has already begun to understand the difference in Sam's cries – she can tell if it is a cry of pain/upset, or another for hunger and a third when he is just whingy. She says that she has yet to understand his tired cry.

Sam at 2 months old:

Rachel puts Sam down on his mat and at first he becomes agitated, but when he focuses in on her face and hears her voice he settles and does so even more when Rachel takes hold of his hands and holds them to his side. Later, Sam gets agitated but the instant that Rachel interacts with him he settles. He responds to the sound of her voice and to her face when he focuses in.

Sam at 4 months old:

Rachel gave him to me and he showed no reaction to me holding him but he could see and hear Rachel.

Sam at 7 months old:

As Rachel had to get something from the buggy, I held Sam for her. He did not bother about being with me but interestingly he stared hard at me at the same time, feeling my face as if mapping my features. All the time, he was aware that his mother was still in view.

Sam at 10 months old:

He loved having lots of attention on holiday – he latched on to Neil's dad quite happily. He went down to the shop with him every morning – to the extent where he began to expect things so that when they went to the shop and Neil's dad was buying the bread and the croissants, he was looking round as if to say, I normally have one of these on the way home and you haven't given me any yet! He quite got into the routine by the end of it.

Sam at 19 months old:

This observation was carried out the day after Rachel had done some external training work and Sam had stayed at home with his grandparents. Rachel talks about the effects of that day out:

> Yesterday was probably the first time that I have left him to go and do something. He has not bothered about it when Neil's mum and dad have been here normally. The minute I got my handbag and started to get my

(Continued)

(Continued)

coat, he was in a real temper and that was right up until I went. When I got back he seemed fine, quite happy to see me. But this morning has been different. When Neil came in I think he assumed that I was going to go again and then I went out and he was in the kitchen and he doesn't normally notice what I am doing – he got upset. Maybe he is just a little more aware. Last night he wasn't bothered when I went out of the room. But it was like he associated that we had just been to school and that is what happened yesterday, they arrived and then I went off and today Neil arrived – just that early morning association.

The importance of attachment theory came to the fore again in 2006 when Sir Richard Bowlby, son of John Bowlby, wrote an open letter that was printed in the national press (*Daily Telegraph*, 21/10/06, p. 25, www.telegraph.co.uk). In this letter, he openly targeted group daycare as a place where babies and toddlers are exposed to environments which cause high levels of stress. He goes on to describe a situation where, because babies and toddlers are experiencing different carers, they are in danger of not forming attachments.

Although there have always been concerns about the high turnover of staff within day care settings, it is unusual for staff to move rooms in order to avoid attachments being formed. On the contrary there are occasions where the staff or 'key persons' have moved with the children to the next room in order to ensure consistency of care. In his conclusion, Sir Richard Bowlby recognizes that childcare with a secondary attachment figure – for example, a childminder, grandmother or other relative – is a more positive model, and that childcare arrangements should recognize the role of attachment in the emotional development of babies and young children (*Daily Telegraph*, 21/10/06, p. 25, www.telegraph.co.uk).

Attachment theory assumes that if a child is insecure in the first year, this continues for life. Perhaps then this is a reason for not only maintaining the present right to a year's maternity leave but for extending this to a right to a year's *paid* maternity leave. An argument against this extended maternity leave is related to the fact that frequently babies are not accessing out-of-home day care provision until they are much older, which many practitioners believe causes more problems when it comes to separation. Practitioners often comment on how it is more difficult to settle babies when they are older as they experience more anxiety at separation than when they were a few months old. This is in line with the thinking of Bowlby

(1989) and Ainsworth (1969) when they conducted their research into attachment theory.

Bruer (1999, p. 58) questions this assumption by recognizing that 'what matters is early experience plus whatever happens afterward', and, unlike Belsky (2001), he argues that there is no research that links attachment theory to brain development. Fonagy (2001, p. 30) states: 'Evidence that suggests that attachment is the foundation for later adaptation is neither reliable nor consistent'. And Eliot (1999, p. 313) extends this further when she writes '... that quality childcare (and quality parenting) is the key to protecting babies' brain and emotional development'.

These challenges to attachment theory are raised in research into children who have experienced extreme levels of deprivation. Research into the effects of deprivation on the children discovered in Romanian orphanages, who were later adopted, showed that children are resilient and that depending on the duration of deprivation, there is cognitive catch-up. The findings are not conclusive and, as O'Connor et al. (2000, p. 388) discuss, further study needs to be made to discover the future effects on these children's development.

The research appears to challenge the theory that deprivation has a lasting effect on children's cognitive development: 'The marked catch-up observed in most children appears to be at odds with the (above) emphasis on early experiences' (O'Connor et al., 2000, p. 388).

The Effective Provision of Pre-School Education (EPPE) *Project 1997–2004* (Sylva et al., 2003), a longitudinal study of children's development between 3 and 7 years of age in the UK, has been looking at the effects of pre-school attendance on children's long-term development. The findings from the pre-school period (Sylva et al., 2003) reflect on the findings to date. Although the study started when the children were 3, some of these findings have reflected on children's patterns of care before that age. Their findings show that an early attendance (between 2 and 3 years of age) in some form of pre-school has a link with cognitive attainment and social development and that these benefits continue at the end of Key Stage 1.

When looking at those children who had no pre-school experience, there was evidence of poorer cognitive attainment, sociability and concentration upon entry to school. The research recognized that parental intellectual levels had no bearing on children's outcomes. What was of greatest importance was what parents, and mothers in particular, did with their children in terms of interaction, offering activities such as painting and drawing, going on visits and giving children regular opportunities to play with their friends. This is reflected in the care offered by childminders.

In England, the *Families, Children and Childcare* (FCCC) study focuses on the relationship between childcare and outcomes for children. The FCCC concludes in its rationale for the study (Sylva et al., at www.familieschildrenchildcare.org, p. 10): 'Whatever the nature of the care provided, it is the quality of parent–child relationships which shape developmental outcomes.' The study sets out to learn more about families in the UK who are making childcare choices. It is these choices and the home environment which finally influence later outcomes for children.

In order to address the issues, the study recruited mothers from two centres in London and Oxford, antenatally and post-natally. The study recognizes that there are many variables when studying outcomes for children: gender, the individual child and his relationship with his mother, when and for how long the child is in care and in which setting and with which practitioner. These variables mean that it is impossible to come to a definite and reliable conclusion.

When looking at mothers' decisions concerning employment and out-of-home care, Leach et al. (2006a and b) found that the warmth of carers and the quality of their interactions, along with the length of sessions and location, were of importance. In the study group, the most common type of childcare accessed was a childminder, because these mothers thought that group day care was inappropriate for young babies. It was felt that childminders, nannies or relatives could offer a more individual approach to caring.

Key to questioning attachment theory where children are in out-of-home settings is the relationship between the setting and the parents. Practitioners need to be non-judgemental towards parents and they need to recognize the importance of their role in trying to establish a strong bond with the baby. As Gerhardt (2004, p. 23) states:

> Babies need a caregiver who identifies with them so strongly that the baby's needs feel like hers. If she feels bad when the baby feels bad, she will then want to do something about it immediately, to relieve the baby's discomfort – and this is the essence of regulation.

Practitioners, who work long hours and are underpaid, have to establish the same strong bond with parents in recognition of the importance of practitioners and parents really working together (Langston, 2006).

What is recognized in the literature on attachment theory is that it is the quality and consistency of care that has effects on the child's relationships and social development. If a child receives good quality care in an out-of-home setting and the adult support is consistent, then the child is able to develop attachment to more than one caregiver.

> What does seem to be true is that attachment relationships remain stable as long as the childcare situation, and the circumstances of the parents and family, remain stable. (Bruer, 1999, p. 184)

Attachment is related to care giving and it is here that the role of the mother is raised. Mothers are traditionally seen as a child's primary caregiver. Although in recent years fathers have played a greater role in the parenting of their children, it has always been the woman who has taken on the primary role: '"parenting" – which is, within current social arrangements, usually mothering' (Burman, 1994, p. 33).

The bonding between mother and child is often seen from the outside as an automatic process but, as Leach (2010, p. 43) describes it, it is a relationship that builds up over time:

> Mothers and midwives have always known that while bonding may happen in a flash of welcoming recognition at the moment of delivery ('Hello baby, I didn't realise it was you') the bonds between mother and baby more usually evolve over hours or days and may not build up to full strength for several weeks.

Leach recognizes the complexity of forming an attachment, even between mother and child, which is why it is so important for settings to get their relationships with the child and her family right.

Key persons

As this key relationship between mother and child develops and becomes secure, it is important that it continues as the baby transitions into forming further relationships. Babies and children are capable of forming multiple relationships, just as we as adults do, but in their infancy we need to pay special attention to them. When a child is looked after by a childminder, the key person relationships between parents, child and childminder are clear to see but it becomes more complex when babies and young children attend day care settings. The responses from parents and practitioners which follow reveal this complexity. It is hard for this three-way relationship to develop when staff work in shifts, when there is a high staff turnover and when there is a lack of commitment from any of the parties involved. Elfer et al. (2003) recognize this when they describe the relationship as:

> ... being special for the children, helping them manage throughout the day, thinking about them, getting to know them well, and sometimes worrying about them too – all of which help a child to make a strong link between home and nursery.

There is recognition in the following parent interview data that it is the quality of the caregiving and the forming of additional bonds that is of great importance. It is with this recognition in mind that I asked parents in the interview about the 'key person' system and the ways in which they felt that their children had formed relationships with the adults. I found it revealing that when asked about the 'key person' system (as discussed by Elfer et al., 2003), parents at one of the nurseries were ambivalent about it and many were unaware of its existence. Some of the parents refer to seeing information or lists up on the walls of the nursery:

> On the list on the wall it's got a list of carers for each child, Tim has got a girl called M I think but I don't know who she is. (Mother of Tim)

> They've not introduced me to it but I've seen the notice up about the key worker stuff but I've not had any talk about it. I don't know what the procedure is. It depends who is in the room to give me feedback. (Mother of Josh)

Other parents recall that they were told about the 'key person' system and had heard it mentioned once they were in the nursery, but did nothing more to find out how it operated or who their child's 'key person' was:

> They have a key worker system I believe, I don't know who the key worker is but they did tell me in detail about it. (Mother of Ben)

> They do but they don't tell you whose Mark's is. She did say do you want one of us to be his key worker because we've got the same number each so I said you decide it as you decide it. But I don't really know who it is. (Mother of Mark)

> I don't think when I first started they had a key worker. (Mother of James)

> One of two, because one of the other girls doesn't speak very much, but I couldn't tell you her name. I'm only aware of it because it does say on the door what is the key worker. (Mother of Maisie)

The parents in the other nursery had a different response to the question about key working. They were aware of its existence and knew what it involved:

> D is her key worker but she seems to go to other people. I did speak to another friend who said that their daughter got into a relationship with a key worker and when she left she was at a loose end and she cried all the time. Melanie only cries when I go to pick her up. If I knew what she [D] was doing that would be good. (Mother of Melanie)

Parents in both settings, however, were able to discuss the relationships that their children had made with adults in general and also to talk about how well the adults knew their children:

> They know his moods, yes they know him. At the end of the day he spends quite a lot of time with them. (Mother of Martin)

> They seem to know him well. Two people look after him all of the time and yes I have been quite pleased by how they are with him. (Mother of Dan)

> I think they know her very well. (Mother of Harriet)

Within these responses, there were no signs of jealousy from the parents about the relationships that their children had formed with the adults in the setting.

> I was very surprised, they knew when she was tired. They just knew. I don't know how, it was really weird. It was a good thing but the way they just kind of read her and just knew everything just like they had been with her weeks and weeks and weeks. (Mother of Harriet)

> As well as they could get to know them when there's so many there. (Mother of Maisie)

> I think they do know him well because he has now graduated to the toddler group; before he was in the baby group and they say he is happy to go in there. In the morning when you drop he's happy to go in there. There is no remorse. (Mother of Ben)

In both settings, there is a 'key person' system but the comments from the sample interviewed showed a difference in what the staff in each setting thought was the reason for having such a system. At one nursery, the three members of staff interviewed all saw the main reason for having such a system to be for administrative purposes:

> I think if you didn't have one [key worker system] when it came to doing your development chart there would be one person ending up all the time doing it. Basically it's just to share that work load out so that not just one person is doing it all the time. (Practitioner)

> … we don't necessarily say that you, P, are the only person who can look after these children. We don't work it like that, its just basically to write up the stages of development folders and the observations. We make it our point to make sure theirs is done and if we've got any queries you know about their development then we will be the ones to sort that but we don't say that is your child. (Practitioner)

> So I do think it's important and also for the children because if you have 10 children and one member of staff says I'll do P today and then someone might not have heard that and then the next day someone else will say I'll do an observation on P. So on Tuesday and Wednesday you get two observations on P and none of the other children. You need to know who you are focusing on and why. It just makes it easier all round for the team I think. (Practitioner)

This lack of understanding about the role of the 'key person' recognizes the need for training around this issue. When one of these practitioners was asked if she felt the system was important, she gave the following response:

> If I'm honest, no. Because I think the whole room works as a team, the staff work as a team. The way they look after the children is all done as part of a team. So I don't see why staff should have to be split down with the children to do with the individual child. I think it would be better if it was just done as a team and everyone had the same care. (Practitioner)

Perhaps this comment indicates why the 'key person' system in this nursery was not recognized by any of the parents interviewed, and why some of these parents felt that there was a lack of communication between setting and home.

In one nursery, the responses from the staff indicated that they have a better understanding of the 'key person' system and that because of this they recognize the importance of parents' need to form relationships with the staff. Also, it is interesting to note that in these responses there is a consistency about how the 'key person' system works. The first practitioner commented on its use for administrative purposes, as well as recognizing the importance of an in-depth knowledge of individual children:

Yes. We have all got children each. I have got three. We are doing different planning for them – so if any of the parents have got any problems they can come to us. It's when it comes to planning – its not like they are our children and all we do is change their nappies or only feed those children. It's much more to do with the paper work. It is important because you can know three children more in depth – if they have any problems then you can look into it further than when looking at nine babies. (Practitioner)

The remaining comments make more mention of forming partnerships and relationships with parents:

Yes. In the baby room we have four each and we give parents a letter about us so that they know all about us and our training and if they have any problems or they want to ask anything we should know because they are our children. It is definitely a good system. Because you get to know the parents on a name basis. You get to talk to them. They talk to you. Some of the parents don't know how it works; we had one mother who thought I had to do his nappy or whatever because I was his key worker. (Practitioner)

Yes. I have got four children and it's like if the parents want to speak to a certain member of staff, it is hard for them to get to know all of them. So if they have a problem they speak to us about it. It is good to have one and it does work. It is good to build up the relationships, like at the end of the day you can tell what sort of day their child has had. If they have got something to tell you they will make the time. (Practitioner)

Yes. We get four each, sometimes more. Then if the parents have got any problems then they will come to us. Yes, I think it is nice for the parents to interact with us, so that they know who to go to. (Practitioner)

The confusion that exists within day care settings over the validity of this approach is recognized by Nutbrown and Page (2008 p. 98) when they comment, '... we are left with the question as to whether all practitioners and managers have yet been able to understand and interpret the subtleties of the role of the key person and to put this complex role into practice'. It is the duty of managers to ensure that their staff teams and their parents understand the place of this crucial role and its purpose in giving babies and young children emotional security.

Leadership and management and the key person system

As mentioned in the opening chapter, the two nurseries that I used in my research differed in the way in which they operated and also in the way in which they were managed. As the comments from the interviews with the practitioners about the key person system above illustrate, the practitioners at one of the nurseries were clear that they could support each other and that the manager was also supportive of the way in which relationships with children were developed through the existence of an effective 'key person' model. The other nursery had no such clear philosophy or ethos, and the staff team did not feel supported at critical times. It is crucial that for a key person system to be effective, the setting must have a commitment to it and it must be part of the organizational philosophy and ethos. For the approach to be effective, parents must be informed about it and its benefits for them and their children. Managers have a responsibility to support their staff not only to understand and implement the system, but also to support them when this becomes difficult. Perhaps it is the difference in definition between Leader and Manager that can cause this dilemma, as these roles are often seen as interchangeable within the day care sector. As Whalley (2011) defines them, the role of the Manager is to plan and organize the workforce, as opposed to the Leader who is the inspirational person who builds the team and empowers them to move forwards. It is hard to separate these roles, but perhaps this was one of the intended aims of the role of the Early Years Professional, which will be discussed later in this chapter.

Although the key person system is now embedded in statutory legislation (DfES, 2007), practitioners are still often reluctant to implement it, commenting that they know all of the children well. Some settings still operate a system where one person changes all of the nappies, and yet they would insist that they have a key person system. Ofsted enforces the system through legislation, but this is interpreted by many settings as an onerous piece of administration which does not have an impact on their practice or on their relationships with babies and young children. I would suggest that many settings which are identified in Ofsted reports as having such a system are merely paying lip service to the term key person.

Training and qualifications

As interaction between adults and babies and young children is important, value has to be placed on the qualifications and training of the adults involved. Out of the seven members of staff interviewed at one of the case study day nurseries, one was unqualified, two had NVQ 3 (NVQs assess the skills that candidates demonstrate at work and are available at five levels, from Level 1 for routine jobs, to Level 5 for jobs with complex tasks and substantial responsibility), one had a Cache diploma, which is a two-year course leading to a nationally recognized qualification in childcare, and three had obtained their NVQ 2, two of whom were studying for their level 3. One of the seven practitioners interviewed was a male, who was unqualified. Each member of staff interviewed was asked whether they felt that their training had given them a good understanding of child development. The responses from two of the staff showed that they felt the NVQ approach where they gained their qualification was a good thing, not because it meant that they gained a greater understanding of child development but because they did not want to learn in the classroom.

> It has yes because I did it within a setting not sat in a classroom, just read out of books. I actually did it in the nursery setting. You get more hands-on experience whilst you are training, not just reading how to do it out of a textbook and just going into a nursery setting where it is done differently anyway. (Practitioner)

> It has. I think there was a lot of written work to take in and in my opinion I thought a lot of learning about how children work is to actually do the practical side of it which is why I did a modern apprenticeship. I didn't want to sit in a classroom five days a week writing, there was a lot of written work but at the same time there was the practical side to it. (Practitioner)

Other practitioners mentioned the fact that they gained support from the settings where they were working and that this, along with the college input, gave them a better understanding of child development:

> Yes. I have got that from both the nursery and the college. (Practitioner)

The next comment recognizes the difficulties that practitioners have in trying to fit in training and assignments when they are working full time in a setting. When practitioners are training whilst in a setting, the question of quality arises; in-setting training can only be as good as the setting. If practice is bad in a setting, then the student is not being exposed to quality childcare practice.

> Yes. Both the training and the nursery. It's good to be working in the nursery as you are training. I am doing my NVQ 3 now. I have been doing this since I was 16. I feel that it is dragging on a bit. It's once a

week when we are going to college so we do an early shift in the nursery so I don't get home until 10.00 pm. I work weekends as well so I have no time to do the college work. It's like fitting it in where I can. (Practitioner)

A challenge for colleges is how they ensure that settings employing these students are of the highest quality.

One of the practitioners commented on the importance for her of the theoretical study that she did at college:

I think the cache route is better because of the work that I'd do with the curriculum because I was in college four days a week – so I did more of the work but I did placements as well. (Practitioner)

For me, underpinning knowledge of child development is crucial to any professional qualification, and in my experience many of the practitioners who have gained some of the work-based NVQ qualifications have little or no confidence in what and how babies and young children should be learning at different stages of development. Perhaps this is why Tickell (2011), in her review of the EYFS (DfES, 2007), recommends that the milestones of development for 24-month-old children be set out clearly alongside the development matters statements.

One of the positive outcomes, for many, of the EYFS (DfES, 2007) has been the increased professionalism of childminders. This occupation has traditionally been seen as the second-class citizen of the childcare workforce, but over the last 10 years of my experience of working within local authorities, the status of childminders has been growing. Even in Sweden, with its high quality childcare and high status for practitioners, the work of the childminder is regarded as inferior. Here the childminder is called a family daycare provider and is usually employed by the local authority. In Sweden, this form of childcare is in decline. I feel, however, that more recently childminders are eager to develop their skills and improve the quality of care and learning that they offer to babies and young children. They are in a unique position to develop relationships with parents, and to be able to offer a home environment, as discussed in the next chapter.

Vocation or job?

Linked to the practitioners' training is the question of why they had chosen to go into childcare in the first place. Three of those interviewed gave the typical response that it was a liking of children that made them choose this as a career:

> Well, I had such a great experience in school with a great teacher. I am also the oldest, I got used to having babies around, I wanted to carry it on. When I was in primary school the teachers were just so kind I just wanted to do it. (Practitioner)

> Because I enjoy being with young children. (Practitioner)

> Because I like working with children and I didn't want to work in an office. (Practitioner)

One responded that she 'fell' into childcare because of her need to find a job:

> To be honest, it was lack of money and I needed to get into a job quickly. I was looking through a newspaper and I found one in another nursery and I realize that I am a big kid at heart and I really enjoyed it, so I stuck at it and I started on my qualification. (Practitioner)

I also asked what the practitioners felt were their greatest strengths in working with children. The responses ranged from comments about being patient to considering themselves like children and that this quality enabled them to interact and forge better relationships with the children in their care. Three of the practitioners related this to their own child-like qualities:

> I'm like a big kid myself. (Practitioner)

> I am bubbly with them. (Practitioner)

> Well, I'm a big kid myself so I can relate to children. (Practitioner)

Others thought that an empathy with children was important, but that patience was the ultimate strength needed to work with young children:

> Patience is one. Being firm, when they have a tantrum being able to sit down with them and talking to them. I actually really get on well with the children so I reckon it is talking to them. (Practitioner)

> I'm crazy. I think you have to be crazy to work with children, you have to be weird. I must admit I do have quite a bit of patience and I think that helps a lot. But generally because I'm just happy. Obviously, if a child sees someone around who's happy, who's willing to sit down and play with them. (Practitioner)

This last comment is something which is a crucial element of quality practice. If adults are seen to be enjoying being with and interacting with babies and young children, the quality of interaction is of a higher standard. Sadly, sometimes adults are seen who look as if they are bored and this has a contagious effect on the children in their care.

The comments from these practitioners are reflective of the low status of the profession and the value, or lack of it, that they put on their impact on the development of babies and young children. Why is it that girls, in particular, are encouraged to go into childcare if they are unlikely to achieve educationally, as it is seen as a profession where all you need is a liking for children? Young children are precious and yet society is happy for them to be cared for by practitioners with low academic achievements. Society is also happy for these practitioners, who work particularly long hours for low pay, to work in a profession which is not highly regarded. This is reflected in the comments by Aubrey (2011) when she states: 'A major concern focuses on government's reluctance to rationalize the early childhood workforce in terms of qualifications, pay and conditions'. Until we as a society demand that childcare becomes a fully recognized profession with improved pay and working conditions and a high quality career path, the standard of childcare in the UK will not be of the highest quality.

Men in the early years workplace

One of the practitioners interviewed was male and his comments about his strengths are interesting in that he relates them to his gender:

> When I worked in Stoke my supervisor said no one knew what to say to you when you first walked in. I said, what, I go to the toilet a few times a day, like you I have to eat. I breathe, I sleep, I do my hair in the morning, aftershave you know – there is such a stigma about being a guy, I'm just myself, I don't put on any barriers or false pretences. Whether that's strengths or not it is sort of. (Practitioner)

Although there has been a drive to attract more men into early years, very few male practitioners are encountered within this profession.

These comments from a male practitioner are echoed by comments made by one of the fathers interviewed:

> At first I was worried, I thought it's a lad, what's going on here, and from a bloke's point of view ... why is he with kids? I still don't see why he's there but it's fantastic. A good male role model. A bit of rough and tumble. I think he is better with the older ones, I can't see him with babies. (Father of Mark)

The influence of male role models in early years is sadly lacking, especially when one considers the impact that they can have. Hopefully, this reaction to male workers will change as fathers become more involved in the care of their babies; not because it is expected of them but because they want to be.

The following two case studies illustrate the value of young children and babies being supported by carers of both sexes.

 Case study 6: Mark at 2½ years old

- Mark goes to find the other adult who is now on the floor. He climbs onto his back. He appears to enjoy being close to the male worker and snuggles in to play closer with the adult.
- He begins to interact with the adult by building the cogs – he laughs and responds to the adult's questions.
- Mark doesn't appear to like it when another boy gets close to the adult. This is the same child who was playing with the adult when they were at the dough table.
- Whilst in this area with the adult, Mark became interested in a book – again, the adult does not follow this up.

Reflection:

Mark appears to be a very boisterous boy and the adults respond to this but they seem to miss that he has good concentration skills, and that he has an interest in things which could be extended. I would suggest that by the way in which he handles books he enjoys stories and looking at books – again, something not followed up by the adults in the room. Mark also has a sensitive side which is not encouraged – the rough and tumble is accepted and extended, but Mark enjoys the closeness of those adults that he engages with, especially the male worker, and is upset when others interrupt these 'special' moments.

Case study 7: Sam at 6 months old

Rachel comments that Sam likes a rough and tumble time. She comments that Neil is good at this, but that she doesn't do it very well. Is there a difference in the way that Neil does rough and tumble?

> Definitely. Even if I do it, it hasn't got the same effect or the same strength to it – there is just something about it that I am not as rough as Neil would be. Throwing him in the air: I do it, but I am probably more cagey about it and it hasn't got the same excitement factor. I do try to do it, because I know that he enjoys it but he doesn't laugh as much as when Neil does it.

The involvement of men in child rearing and childcare can only have a positive impact on babies and young children. Without being stereotypical, the two genders bring different qualities to their interactions with children.

Continuing professional development

Continuing professional development (CPD) is key to improving the quality of care that babies and young children experience in out-of-home settings. The national government and local authority agendas have established different levels of CPD for a range of practitioners. Much of this at local authority level is around statutory requirements, such as safeguarding and first aid. There is a danger that practitioners can see this as the only elements of training that they should access. Those practitioners who attend training which develops their skills and challenges their thinking are those who bring about a change in the quality of their practice. Many practitioners have now attended a range of training, and are ready to develop through gaining higher levels of qualifications.

When budgets are under pressure, it can mean that the local authorities' commitment to offering free training is threatened. If the possibility of charging for training becomes a reality, it is possible that many will forgo what is seen as the 'fun training', those training opportunities which are about reflecting on practice and encouraging practitioners to engage with new ways of working, in favour of keeping their statutory training up to date.

With this in mind, the UK Labour government (1997–2010) allocated £52 million to the Children's Workforce Development

Council (CWDC) to develop and deliver the training for Early Years Professional (EYP) status. This status was intended to make the practitioner responsible for leading on and delivering the EYFS in all settings. The rationale for the development of this status was based on research evidence from the EPPE Project (1997–2004), where it was concluded that the highest levels of learning and a raising of quality occur when the practitioner has higher qualifications. Within the private, voluntary and independent (PVI) sector, this has always been a concern. In this sector, the majority of practitioners work long hours with poor pay and working conditions. There is a need to raise the levels of qualification to level 3 (most practitioners have only achieved level 2) if all children are to receive high quality learning and care. There is also a need for those who are qualified to a higher level (normally teachers) to obtain knowledge and experience of working with children under the age of 3, if they are to become involved in delivering the EYFS (DfES, 2007) within Children's Centres and in leading and supporting practice in the private, voluntary and independent sector.

Traditionally, practitioners in the early years have been young with low levels of qualifications, and this has brought about much criticism of their abilities to interact and work with babies and very young children. Frequently, those practitioners who are felt to be the 'weakest' are put into the baby rooms, almost as part of a damage limitation exercise. This attitude shocks and upsets me, as I feel that the most capable practitioners should be working with our very young children; after all, the baby room is probably the most demanding, physically and mentally, in the whole nursery. What is most upsetting is when some practitioners view being placed in the baby room as a demotion and respond by describing babies as 'boring'. This attitude needs to be monitored and addressed by managers; some of the most successful nurseries are those which have given great consideration to staffing the younger rooms, and perhaps this is why they are successful.

Working with babies and young children can challenge those practitioners who have received higher-level training. As Recchia and Shin (2010) found in their study of teachers' experiences of working with children under 3, this age range is challenging, demanding and needs a different type of support and interaction to help them develop.

I have worked with a group of practitioners who have gained EYP status as a continuum of their CPD after graduating at degree level. We have established a forum where they can network and share elements of their practice. These practitioners have been comprised of day nursery owner-managers, nursery practitioners, pre-school playgroup leaders, childminders, independent school teachers, local authority consultants and Children's Centre teachers and workers. Many of these practitioners work with the older children, and we have used our forum to give them all professional development, especially with regard to the younger children (see Case study 8).

As I have worked with this group of practitioners, I have come to value and respect their experience, expertise, commitment and motivation to continually develop their practice and raise its quality. Four of the nurseries at which these practitioners are based have had Ofsted inspections with 'Outstanding' outcomes, and there is an expectation that more will follow. It is with this in mind that I hope that EYP status does not disappear in government restructuring.

Internationally, the qualification requirements for adults working in the early years are gradually improving. In Australia, the plan is to have the following qualifications in place by January 2020:

- Two early childhood teachers, or another suitably qualified leader, will need to be in attendance all of the time when long day care and pre-school services are being provided to more than 80 children.
- Two early childhood teachers, or another suitably qualified leader, will need to be in attendance at least half of the time when long day care and pre-school services are being provided to 60 children or more.

In New Zealand, they are introducing a professional registration requirement for all teachers in teacher-led Early Childhood Education services, such as those already in place in the schools sector and kindergartens by 2012. This also includes coordinators in home-based care services.

It seems that the model of early years professionalism, which is well established in the Scandinavian countries, is spreading because research has recognized the importance of children interacting with practitioners with a higher level of qualification. It is important that such developments continue in the UK, so that the progress made in increasing qualifications in the last five years is continued.

As the following case study illustrates, the graduate forum that we have established is highly valued within the Local Authority (LA), and demonstrates the value of raising the qualifications of the early years work force.

Case study 8

The EYP forum was established in November 2007 and has expanded as more practitioners have gained the status. The Forum meets twice a term; one day is set aside for CPD and the other is a lunchtime gathering for networking and sharing new practice and ideas. The Forum is now chaired and led by the group, with the Local Authority acting as facilitator. Its achievements to date are: terms of reference, a job description, an EYP library and the opportunity to have access to the following high level CPD:

1 Schemas for Babies
2 Learning Outdoors
3 Communication Friendly Spaces
4 Mathematics for Under-3s

All EYPs are given the opportunity to access conferences and further training. A group of EYPs attended the Communication Friendly Spaces conference and others attended the Aspect 2009 conference, where they heard Ferre Laevers talk about experiential learning. A group of five EYPs have embarked on their Masters degree; the course was free at the time of their involvement and they were given a bursary for books. As part of the Forum's development, the LA have created an EYP room on its learning platform so that its members can share practice and information via the internet. A sub-group was established, to conduct some action research on environments for the under 3s, which has resulted in a document following their stories and describing their achievements.

Quality professional development training is expensive, and so many future plans for this group have had to be altered. On a positive note, because this group is proactive they have decided to continue to meet twice a term without the funding to cover their costs and to request that the LA provide them with this additional challenge from its highly qualified and experienced officers.

The future of the EYP status and further development of the early years workforce is fluid at the time of writing, but in my opinion EYP status has been a valuable development which has definitely raised the standard of practitioners and has begun to give the workforce a structure and professional development pathway; all it needs is for the status to continue and for the pay and working conditions to reflect the importance that must be given to people who work with and care for the most valuable members of our society. Encouraging, however, are the recommendations from Tickell (2011) when she stresses the strengthening of the qualifications to maintain their quality and continuing to promote the work started in creating a graduate workforce.

 Questions for reflection

- What is the ethos and philosophy of your practice and/or setting on the implementation of the key person system?
- How does your practice support practitioners to become effective key persons?
- Consider how the roles of Leaders and Managers are defined within your setting. Reflect on how these different roles impact on the quality of the setting.

Further reading

Allen, G. and Duncan-Smith, I. (2010) *Early Intervention: Good Parents, Great Kids, Better Citizens*. Available at: www.centreforsocialjustice.org.uk/client/downloads/EarlyInterventionpaperFINAL.pdf
This cross-political party paper looks at the radical social policy of 'Early Intervention', outlining how to break the intergenerational cycle of underachievement.

Elfer, P., Goldschmied, E. and Selleck, D. (2003) *Key Persons in the Nursery: Building Relationships for Quality Provision*. London: David Fulton.
This is a key text which offers practitioners and managers advice and support in developing their own key person system.

Bowlby, J. (1989) *The Making and Breaking of Affectional Bonds*. Oxon: Routledge.
A collection of lecture essays spanning the 20-year work of John Bowlby, which provides an introduction to his work on attachment and loss.

Aubrey, C. (2011) *Leading and Managing in the Early Years*, 2nd edn. London: Sage.
This book investigates the role of Leaders across the different areas of the early years sector, and has some important findings when looking at multi-agency teams.

References

Ainsworth, M. (1969) Object Relations, Dependency, and Attachment: A Theoretical Review of the Infant–Mother Relationship. *Child Development*, 40(4): 969–1025.

Aubrey, C. (2011) *Leading and Managing in the Early Years,* 2nd edn. London: Sage.

Belsky, J. (2001) Developmental Risks (Still) Associated with Early Child Care (Emanuel Miller Lecture), *Journal of Child Psychology and Psychiatry,* 42(7): 845–59.

Bowlby, J. (1989) *The Making and Breaking of Affectional Bonds.* Oxon: Routledge.

Bruer, J. (1999) *The Myth of the First Three Years.* New York: Free Press.

Burman, E. (1994) *Deconstructing Developmental Psychology.* New York: Routledge.

Department for Education and Employment (DfEE) (1998) *Meeting the Childcare Challenge.* London: The Stationery Office.

Department for Education and Skills (DfES) (2007) *Statutory Framework for the Early Years Foundation Stage: Setting the Standards for Learning, Development and Care for Children from Birth to Five.* Nottingham: DfES.

Elfer, P., Goldschmied, E. and Selleck, D. (2003) *Key Persons in the Nursery: Building Relationships for Quality Provision.* London: David Fulton.

Eliot, L. (1999) *Early Intelligence.* London: Penguin.

Fonagy, P. (2001) *Attachment Theory and Psychoanalysis.* New York: Other Press.

Gerhardt, S. (2004) *Why Love Matters: How Affection Shapes a Baby's Brain.* Hove: Brunner-Routledge.

Langston, A. (2006) Why Parents Matter. In L. Abbot and A. Langston (eds), *Parents Matter: Supporting the Birth to Three Matters Framework.* Maidenhead: Open University Press.

Leach, P. (2010) *The Essential First Year: What Babies Need Parents to Know.* London: Dorling Kindersley.

Leach, P., Barnes, J., Malmberg, L., Sylva, K., Stein, A. and the FCCC team (2006a) The Quality of Different Types of Child Care at 10 and 18 months: A Comparison Between Types and Factors Related to Quality. *Early Child Development and Care Volume,* 176(5): 553–73.

Leach, P., Barnes, J., Nichols, M., Goldin, J., Stein, A., Sylva, K., Malmberg, L. and the FCCC team (2006b) Childcare Before Six Months of Age: A Qualitative Study. *Infant and Child Development,* 15(5): 471–502.

Murray, L. and Andrews, L. (2000) *The Social Baby.* Richmond: CP Publishing.

Nutbrown, C. and Page, J. (2008) *Working with Babies and Children: From Birth to Three.* London: Sage.

O'Connor, T.G., Rutter, M., Beckett, C., Keaveney, L., Kreppner, J. and the English and Romanian Adoptees Study Team (2000) The Effects of Global Severe Privation on Cognitive Competence: Extension and Longitudinal Follow-up. *Child Development,*17(2): 376–90.

Recchia, S. and Shin, M. (2010) 'Baby Teachers': How Pre-service Early Childhood Students Transform their Conceptions of Teaching and Learning through an Infant Practicum. *Early Years,* 30(2): 135–45.

Sylva, K., Meluish, E., Sammons, P., Siraj-Blatchford, I., Taggart, B. and Elliot, K. (2003) *The Effective Provision of Pre-School Education (EPPE) Project: Findings from the Pre-School Period* (Research Brief No: RBX15-03). London: DfES Publications.

Tickell, C. (2011) *The Early Years: Foundations for Life, Health and Learning. An Independent Report on the Early Years Foundation Stage to Her Majesty's Government.* London: DfE. Available at www.education.gov.uk/tickell review

Whalley, M. (2011) Leading and Managing in the Early Years. In L. Miller, and C. Cable (eds), *Professionalization, Leadership and Management in the Early Years.* London: Sage.

Useful websites

www.familieschildrenchildcare.org

www.minedu.govt.nz/NZEducation/EducationPolicies/EarlyChildhood. aspx

www.deewr.gov.au/Earlychildhood/Policy_Agenda/Quality/Pages/ EarlyYearsLearningFramework.aspx

4 The Physical Environment

This chapter will:

- discuss the organization of the physical environment
- challenge thinking about age grouping in day care settings
- discuss children's exposure to challenging resources
- discuss how to create a home-like environment
- look at how the physical environment, indoors and outdoors, can be planned to meet the needs of babies and young children
- discuss using colours to both calm and stimulate.

The physical environment plays a crucial role in the learning and development of babies and young children and is strongly linked to the other environments already discussed. If the adult does not plan an appropriate environment which engages, stimulates and motivates young learners, then they become restless, they do not become involved and they do not persevere. If the environment is not planned with an understanding of child development, then babies and young children will not feel safe and secure and this will have an impact on their emotional development.

Pre-Birth to Three (The Scottish Government, 2010), the Scottish framework, recognizes the importance of the environment when it states '… that babies arrive into the world with their individual personalities, ready to adapt to, and be influenced by their environments'. It is therefore incumbent on us as early years practitioners to ensure that the environments that we create for the babies and young children in our care are of the highest quality and that they support and challenge in all aspects of their learning and development. The dilemma with a lot of the environments that we create for babies and young children is that we use the model of the school and impose it on an environment which is supposed to be about loving and caring as much as it is about learning. At the time, the EYFS (DfES, 2007) revolutionized political thinking by removing the previous barriers between learning and caring and stressing that they were interdependent on one another.

Environments for children under 3 years of age are possibly the most challenging to organize. Practitioners who embrace the philosophy of continuous provision need to do so with a real understanding of the children who spend time in those rooms. It is important to create quiet reflective spaces where young children can enjoy being on their own away from the sometimes over-stimulating environment where they spend most of their time. The skill is to achieve this without over-designing the space to the point that it has no flexibility for children to change it during their play. The environment needs to address the developing needs of children under 3. It should include physical challenge, opportunities for social interaction and an atmosphere which encourages language development, especially listening. Every setting needs a 'listening space', where babies and young children can hear themselves and others talk, thus encouraging children to talk.

Organization of the physical environment

Traditionally, private day nurseries are organized in rooms according to the chronological age of the babies and young children. This means that depending on the size of the nursery, babies and young children can experience many room changes or transitions. Not only do they experience a change of environment, they more often than not experience a change of adult. These transitions and attachment changes – and in some nurseries there can be as many as five moves – can have a negative impact on the emotional wellbeing of babies and young children. When you consider that, as stated previously, many of the babies are entering day nursery between 9 and 12 months old, and leaving to go to a maintained nursery class when they are 3, they are moving five times in under three years; even in our school system children only make this change once a year.

The EYFS welfare regulations state that babies under 2 have to have access to a separate area:

> Except in childminding settings, there should be a separate baby room for children under the age of two, but they should be able to have contact with older children and be transferred to the older age-group after the age of 18 months, or as appropriate for their individual stage of development. (DfES, 2007)

Historically, it has been felt that non-mobile babies should be kept separate from those babies who have begun to toddle. This does mean that this first move of rooms is for developmental reasons but can you imagine a child who is moved on to the next room because of his age? All those friends and social links that have been made are broken as he is sent to another room.

Case study 9: Transition – a parental perspective: Freddie at 20 months old

After a considerable gap, I became a parent for the third time and it was in the hazy few weeks after Freddie's birth that it dawned on me that, unlike many other working mums, I had not considered the childcare I would need to enable me to return to work. As this was unfamiliar to me, I sought the help of a friend who had had twins six months previously; it was on her recommendation and in the comfort that the twins would be attending that I registered Freddie at the same setting. Freddie started nursery in February 2009 and was in the baby room with the twins, and it was through their mum that I got to know other parents and their children. This network was especially important to me in those early days of my return to work. As the babies became mobile and turned 1 [year old], a large group was moved to the toddler room, that is except Freddie. I felt at this time that I lost touch with a group of parents and their children that I had become used to. However, in September 2009, Freddie finally joined the previous group of children, and by now Freddie clearly recognized these children and their parents and would ask for individuals.

It was in November and December 2009 that I noticed the profile of the toddler room had changed and many of the children who Freddie referred to were no longer there, and there was a very young group of babies in their place. I approached Freddie's key worker to ask if certain children had left, but was told that they had moved rooms. I voiced my concerns that Freddie had lost his group of friends, and that he regularly asked about them. It was made clear that it was setting policy for children to only move at the identified transition point, which was 2 years old, and Freddie was four months too young. Initially, I accepted this and Freddie remained in the toddler room; it was when I thought about the situation that I once again approached his key worker to ask if Freddie could be put back with his social group, as I felt this was very important to his personal, social and emotional development. Initially, the setting was reluctant to move Freddie, however I persevered and eventually it was agreed that Freddie could move to the next group earlier than the setting planned.

(Continued)

(Continued)

Looking back, I know that I was right to ask for an earlier transition, based on his needs rather than age, as Freddie had clearly formed strong attachments to the children in this group. His key worker has admitted that, despite initial reservations, Freddie clearly was more than ready for the challenges of the next room and that she often forgets he is one of the youngest. I know that this situation will arise once again as the children he is friendly with move to the pre-school room, but I am more than ready this time to raise the question 'What about Freddie?' and encourage the setting to look at the whole child rather than just their age and to take into account parental knowledge.

The two nurseries which engaged with me in my research were arranged and managed in different ways. One was arranged in what is now the traditional way, with babies and children moving rooms according to their chronological age as opposed to their developmental stage, apart from the move from what is often referred to as 'the baby baby' room. The babies and children were supported when they moved rooms, and they went on gradual visits, usually with their key person to support them. An example of this transition from one physical environment to another is illustrated in the following case study.

 Case study 10: Amy at 15 months old

- Amy walks over to the safety gate which separates the baby room and the toddler room – the adults tell me that she has been having some visits next door. Evidently, she likes it for most of the time and they also tell me that the gradual visits next door will begin properly when she returns from her holidays (she goes away at the end of this week).
- Amy then places herself in front of the gate and sits looking through to the next room for 10 minutes. When she is sitting staring into the next room, she looks lonely and isolated and it is only the process that follows which makes this a positive experience for Amy. When the singing starts next door, Amy starts to join in with the actions. She also twists her dummy in her mouth, as mentioned on previous observations.
- When it is snack time in the toddler room and one of the adults is going through the gate, they hold it open and ask Amy if she would like to go in. Amy gives her answer by crawling through and joining the others for their snack. The adults are very welcoming to her and make a fuss of her as they sit her at the table with the others – drawing the other children's attention

to her presence. When she is sitting at the table, she looks around but appears very content. An adult stays close to her, giving her support. She eats her cake and looks around her. She eats well and properly.

- When she has finished her snack and has got down from the table, Amy returns to the gate to look back into the baby room – as if reassuring herself that those loved adults are still there. They acknowledge her. She stays here for a while as if deciding which way to go – the options are entirely hers.

- Another boy comes in from outside to ask her if she wants to go out – he holds out his hand to her. Amy then takes the adult hand and goes with her but she doesn't want to go out; she wants to go in the ball pool so the adult remains inside with her. Amy does a lot of pointing to indicate what she wants. She also uses facial expressions.

- Amy is in the ball pool but she is also looking outside to see what all of the other children are doing.

- Amy then goes to stand next to the coats and points to a Noddy bag and smiles. She does the same when she walks down the row and spots a Bob the Builder bag – I say 'Is it Bob the Builder?' and she starts to sway as if she is remembering the song.

- Amy goes out but in her own time – she stands in the doorway looking out but then goes back into the room.

The change in Amy's growing confidence is showing everyone that she is now at the next stage of development and that she needs more than she is getting in the baby room – she needs the challenge that the toddler room can give her. The easy way in which she is allowed to make these choices makes this transition from one room to another a positive one.

This case study demonstrates that the physical way in which this nursery is managed is not having a negative impact on the children. Within this nursery, this was the most positive transition observed and perhaps this was because these rooms were only divided by a gate which enabled the babies to see where they were going, as well as giving them the opportunity to still have a relationship with the room, adults and peers that they had just left behind. Also, being given the opportunity to see the next room on a daily basis meant that they knew what was happening in there. The positive observation here was that one of the adults in the older baby room used to spend a lot of time singing with the babies, and during these times many of the younger babies could be observed swaying and attempting to do the actions to the rhymes. Having this visible contact with the next room is also beneficial once the baby or toddler has made the transition; it means that she can return to look back to where she has come from and can still maintain her contact with a much-loved adult and all of her friends.

Many nurseries have to be arranged in this way because of the layout of the building, but there are ways around this, such as having family grouping in each of the rooms. I would also suggest that the case study described is the exception in this type of nursery layout.

The buildings that some nurseries occupy cause some limitations as to how the physical environment can be offered to babies and young children. Nurseries frequently have their rooms arranged by chronological age as opposed to family grouping, resulting in small rooms. This is often dictated by the fact that these buildings are not purpose-built but are domestic houses that have been converted. Many owners are reluctant to knock interior walls down to make larger spaces, so as a consequence many of the rooms are small, and although the settings are abiding to the ratios, the rooms feel cramped and restrictive. When you consider that having nine babies or children under the age of 2 means that there also has to be three adults, the amount of floor space available for exploration is limited.

Mixed age grouping

One day nursery used within my research was situated in the city and was unusual in that it had no access to the outdoors other than when the children were taken out for planned activities. All of the children (aged 0–5) were based in one room with an area sectioned off with a low-level picket fence where the under 2s were cared for. This latter feature meant that when siblings attended the setting, they could remain in contact with one another for the whole day. This nursery offered a more family style of care, so that all of the children were in the same room. There were several reasons why this arrangement of the room had a positive impact on the babies and children who attended. The following case study shows how children can benefit from the presence of older children who engage with them in their play.

 Case study 11: Melanie at 2 years 10 months old

When I arrive, Melanie is playing in the construction area – there are others there, but she is working on her own building a train track. She then goes over to the blocks. She is talking to another girl, asking her if that is OK. She is happy and smiling. She is concentrating on the task. She is completely involved in her chosen activity.

- There is a purpose to her building. She is using the blocks to create height – she says, 'These are very, very tall'.
- She laughs as she acknowledges me to show me how her building is developing.
- She is selecting the blocks for a purpose.
- 'Look at this tower now ….' She repeats this phrase over and over until another girl responds.
- The tower falls down – 'We will have to build it again'.
- She is narrating as she begins to rebuild the tower: 'Oh dear, oh dear. I'll fix it again'.
- She leaves the tower and comes over to say hello to me. She tells me that she brought a friend to nursery.
- She goes to invite another child to come and build with her. The other girl (older) suggests that they make a wobbly chair. Melanie tells me that they are going to build a wobbly chair and they both return to the blocks.
- There is active cooperation – each making suggestions, laughing and consulting with one another.
- They try each other's wobbly chairs to sit on.
- They both invite me to look at each of the chairs they have made.
- A boy comes into the area and says that they have broken his model. There is no confrontation and he leaves.
- The girls then return to building a chair together – it breaks.
- Melanie is talking all the time.
- They now make a bench-like seat but it isn't that strong.
- They begin to build it again in another way. They are really persevering. It falls down and they laugh.
- There are other girls around but they just stand and watch the two girls building.
- The older girl is leading the play, but Melanie is making a good contribution to the building and the planning. The older girl is challenging Melanie's play and moving her forward.
- The music plays and they both go into the book corner with the others.
- Melanie goes to sit on the mat and is listening to what the adult has got to tell them all. The adult is telling them about the structure of the day and the environment. Melanie is told that she can go and return to her play. The two girls go over to the puzzle table.
- Again, Melanie is really concentrating on the activity and is involved. If a piece doesn't fit, she tries it again in another place. She turns the pieces round to fit. The pieces have numbers on but she doesn't use the numerals to sequence them in order. A boy wants to join in and this interrupts her concentration. She is happy to try until she is successful. She is not frustrated when it doesn't work.
- She turns to tell me that no. 1 is missing and this stops her involvement with the puzzles.

Vygotsky's theory of the zone of proximal development (ZPD) (1978) was observed in the play of Melanie and an older girl where, because of their different learning styles and levels of development, they were able to challenge each other's learning and thus move it on to the next level. Vygotsky's theories stressed the importance of language in children's learning development (1978). This concept of ZPD was also observed in the following case study when an adult was able to support, challenge and empower Melanie in her learning and development through dialogue and encouragement, to successfully place her blanket in the drawer, something which, when she first attempted it, she could not do.

 Case study 12: Melanie at 20 months old

- The adult suggests that Melanie goes to put her blanket away in one of the drawers. This idea appeals to Melanie and she moves towards the drawers. She begins to pull the drawers out, looking for the right one. She perseveres and stands on tiptoes to look inside the box to see if it is the right one and if there is any room in it.
- Eventually, Melanie decides on one and tries to push the blanket inside – because the drawer is at a higher level, she is unable to push the whole of the blanket and so she just lets it fall out again. She picks it up and tries again.
- The adult who has been observing Melanie's progress suggests that she pulls the drawer out onto the floor and then puts the blanket in. Melanie does this, and is successful in achieving her goal.
- Melanie now turns her attention to pushing the drawer back in. The adult is giving her encouragement, but Melanie is looking at the adult and not where the drawer should be going and as a consequence can't align it properly. With further encouragement and suggestions to look at where the drawer is going, she succeeds.

Although on this occasion it is an adult who moves her learning forward, this is a good example of the power of the zone of proximal development. Vygotsky believed in the importance of adult support and interaction in structuring children's learning, and this case study clearly shows how the adult is moving and challenging the child's understanding through her interaction.

With reference to pre-school children, Vygotsky (1978) stressed the importance of play in a child's development. He asserts that it is through this play that children learn and develop before they access formal education in schools. I would advocate that by caring for children in a mixed age group, we are giving babies and young children the opportunity to experience their out-of-home care in a similar manner to the way they might be cared for at home along with their siblings, who will naturally be of different ages. Many parents make this a conscious choice in looking for day care when they choose to place their children with a childminder, who will be caring for children of different ages in a home environment.

This case study illustrates how one nursery has managed to create a family-style environment.

  Case study 13

This nursery is privately owned and managed, operating from a converted house. It is registered for a maximum of 22 children aged up to 5 years. The babies and children under 2 years of age are in one room, and the children over 2 are in another room which is separated by a gate. Both rooms have direct access to the outdoor environment through French doors.

I was in the under 2s room observing practice; the doors were open and the older children were outside in the garden. The babies were happily playing in the dry sand tray on the floor and with the wet sand in an upright tray alongside the adults. Some of the older children came to look into the baby room. On seeing this, the adults asked some of them if they would like to come in. A few of the older children came in either to play with the babies or to re-acquaint themselves with the resources that were available. These children were talking about how they remembered playing with the different resources when they were in this room. As more of the older children came into the room, it began to take on the feel of being in someone's home, as all of the children were playing with one another and some brothers and sisters were 'touching base' with one another. After a while, the older children drifted off to their own room. This whole episode felt so natural and I spent a very pleasant afternoon observing children who initiated this whole family grouping for a short while.

Recent research has looked at the pros and cons of caring for children in mixed age groups. The Millennium Cohort Study (MCS), which commenced in 2000, is following the lives of 19,000 babies born between 2000 and 2002. This study, *The Quality of Childcare Settings in the Millennium Cohort Study* (QCSMCS), was established to look at a sample of 10,000 millennium children to answer the following research questions:

1 What is the quality of the group childcare settings attended by a sample of Millennium Cohort Study Children?
2 Is there a relationship between the quality of childcare received and children's home background?

A supplementary question which has arisen during the study is:

3 Which centre characteristics are associated with higher or lower quality of provision?

(Mathers et al., 2007, p. 4)

Of interest are some of the findings reported in March 2007 where the age range of children in a room cared for in an out-of-home setting was considered. The report states that when older children were present in a room, there was a better quality of interactions.

The report also noted that when younger children were in the group, there was a negative impact on the quality of the provision. This could be because the younger children make more demands of the adults in respect of their care, and also because having such a range of ages may result in a 'dumbing down' of the provision and resources for the older children.

This issue was also raised in the findings from the *National Evaluation of the Neighbourhood Nurseries Initiative: The Relationships between Quality and Children's Behavioural Development* (Mathers and Sylva, 2007, p. 5). The study was unusual as it focused on children under 3½ years of age and on the quality of the provision.

Within this research, ages of children within rooms was studied. Unlike the *Millennium Cohort Study* (Mathers et al., 2007), it was shown that the quality in mixed age groups was higher. This was because the younger children are challenged in their development by having access to higher-level language and communication, as well as having the opportunity to interact with their role models.

The study, however, did identify that the mixing of ages was likely to have a negative impact on behavioural outcomes for younger children, which creates a dichotomy with the improved cognitive outcomes for these children. This conclusion and the recommendation from this study was that, 'Further research into the impact of mixed age rooms is recommended. They may enhance cognitive ability at the price of emotional security' (Mathers and Sylva, 2007, p. 81).

The mixing of age groups in the city-based nursery where some of the case study observations were conducted was reflective of the findings of the *Millennium Cohort Study* (Mathers et al., 2007), which found that older children could raise the quality of interactions for younger children, albeit at the expense of their emotional development and needs. In order to address these concerns, a setting needs to pay very close attention to the emotional needs and environment of these young children. This challenge to the environmental needs of the younger children can be met when adults are aware of this risk. One setting has addressed this by having 'family corners' within the environment. These corners are spaces where the key person can gather her children together for a more quiet and reflective time. The corner is marked by a collection of photographs, at child level, of the individual children, their families and the key person. These times give the children, especially the youngest children, the opportunity and the space to be part of a small family unit, which helps them to regulate their emotions. It is a safe space for children to go to help them regulate these feelings.

The National Evaluation of the Nurseries Initiative: The Relationship between Quality and Children's Behavioural Development (Mathers and Sylva, 2007, p. 8) also supported this theory, highlighting that '... quality scores were significantly higher in these mixed age groups'.

One of the features of this physical layout within a nursery is that children of all ages can enjoy social times together, as they would in a family home. This was observed when the older children and those babies who were awake had their lunchtimes together. This meant that the younger children could observe the older children and hence have their learning scaffolded.

The proprietor of the nursery where all the children were in one room also laid great importance on the physical layout of the nursery, on the management style and on the practice within the nursery.

> But with being so open plan it is hard to miss anything. If you don't see what is going on you can hear it. (Manager)

In many of the traditional styles of nursery, the manager is accommodated in a room situated away from the main body of the nursery. This can impact on how the manager is involved in the day-to-day running of a nursery. This is illustrated in the comment of the manager of one of the case study nurseries. She is reflective about how she should be monitoring what is going on in the rooms but, because of her other duties and responsibilities, finds it impossible to implement this:

When I've got the time to do it then that is what I would like to do. To find out what is going on because sometimes I feel that I don't know what is going on because I don't get that time to spend in the rooms. (Manager)

Exposure to challenging resources

Having family grouping can also impact on the resources that children of differing ages are exposed to. One of the children that I observed was Sam, a baby cared for at home by his mother. In the many observations of Sam over a three-year period, it became a feature that his mother, Rachel, frequently discussed: the influence of his older siblings on his learning. Through the progress of the observations of Sam, it became evident that his exposure to more challenging resources and his association with older children has meant that he has been challenged in his learning. As a consequence, his development in some areas has been greater than those children who were observed who did not have this exposure.

 Case study 14: Sam

When Sam was a baby, he showed an interest in his brother's remote control. This exposure was further evidenced in the observation when Sam was 2 years 10 months old and he was displaying skills on the computer that had been developed because he had been working alongside his older brother. This development in his motor skills was shown when Sam was 18 months old and he was showing an interest in mark making. Traditionally, older children in day care settings have independent access to resources, but concerns over health and safety often mean that the younger children are offered limited access and then only to resources that are considered 'age-appropriate'.

This was evidenced when Rachel, Sam's mother, talked about his access to the chalk board. When she got it out originally, because Sam was showing an interest in mark making, he appeared to ignore it and any interest was soon lost so she decided to store it away for future use. When she saw that the interest in mark making was not disappearing, she decided to leave the chalk easel out to see if this would have any impact on his usage of this resource. Rachel explains how making this resource accessible impacted on Sam's use of it:

> Because it is there and it is out – I counted the other day and he went to it about 15 times – as he goes past it he will pick up the chalk and use it. It's that bit about getting things out and them not using it so you think they don't like it but it's just perhaps because it isn't there.

Sam's access to more challenging resources such as books, remote control equipment and puzzles has meant that his expertise in these areas has developed at a faster rate. When this was discussed with Rachel in connection with Sam's puzzle play, she commented that the puzzles at the playgroup were too easy for him and that they gave him little challenge and that his level of play in this area could not be catered for within the playgroup environment. Rachel also made the following comment, which reinforces earlier conclusions about the resources and challenges that are offered to children in day care settings:

... nursery staff are similar because they think that is what 2-year-olds do and that is what 2-years-olds play with, but there might be a portion of the group who might be past that but have never been exposed to it and you will never know.

Day nurseries are frequently so inhibited by health and safety restrictions that they are not prepared to let babies and young children engage with resources and equipment that will challenge their learning and development. All environments are prepared to be 'age-appropriate'. If we consider how children cared for at home are exposed to the play resources of their older siblings, just as Sam was, we can see that with the right amount of support we can continue that challenge within some of our settings, just as childminders do in their homes.

Home from home

Many parents choose childcare with a childminder because they want their baby to be cared for in a home environment. This home-from-home atmosphere is obviously much easier for a childminder to achieve than a day care setting so it is sometimes concerning that childminders feel obliged to emulate the day nursery by offering that environment to the children in resource areas. Owing to this unique situation, childminders should stick to the principle of children accessing a home setting. Also, because of the wide range of children accessing the same environment, the environment should be adapted on a moment-by-moment basis, following the children's interests and adapting the environment accordingly. A childminder's setting may look different at different times of the day; she may care for two children under 2 in the morning, pick up a 3-year-old from nursery at lunchtime and then collect three children over the age of 5 from school. It is clear from this example that the environment will have to evolve throughout the day, to cater for all of these different ages, just as a parent would in a family home. It is this home atmosphere which makes the childminder's home a unique choice for parents.

If we consider the day nursery as a place where children are cared for in an environment which is *in loco parentis*, we are considering this environment to be as close to a home as possible. I had a colleague who always affirmed that a day nursery can be nothing other than an institution, and to a certain degree this may be true, but there are things that can be done to make the setting nearer to a home environment.

One way of achieving this is by using adult-sized domestic furniture. Many managers and owners feel that by supplying a sofa or comfortable armchair, they are encouraging their staff to sit down all day long. This assertion is questionable, in that the adults who work in the rooms rarely have the time to take advantage of such an opportunity. What the furniture does provide, however, is the opportunity for babies, adults and children to snuggle in; when they are sharing a book, when they want to sit somewhere quietly with someone special, when they are feeling tired or ill. There is a quotation from the *Birth to Three Matters* framework review of the literature which demonstrates babies and young children's needs for this to occur: '"Snuggling in" gives young babies physical, psychological and emotional comfort' (David et al., 2003). Another advantage of using such furniture is that it gives the adults working in the room access to seating which is more suited to their height and size. If in a day nursery everything is done to optimize hygiene, safety and tidiness because of the numbers of babies and children in the room, then we are doing these children a disservice.

Another problem frequently encountered by nurseries caring for young children is sleeping arrangements. One of the nurseries that took part in my research believed in having cots for babies to sleep in. In line with thinking from physiotherapists, this proprietor believed that babies should be put to sleep in cots to enable them to enjoy a deep sleep and to have the space to move during their sleep. She encountered many parents who wanted their babies to sleep in the buggies or bouncy cradles; this is not an ideal situation as babies are not able to move freely. With this philosophy in mind, the proprietor and I had many a conversation about how having a number of cots in a room gives it the appearance of an institution. Obviously, by hanging mobiles in strategic places and sometimes by hanging drapes around the cots this effect can be minimized. This, however, was a problem we were never able to resolve completely.

Another feature of rooms for babies is the presence of high chairs, which again can give an institutionalized effect if the adults are not skilled in their practice. Frequently, chairs are arranged in a line for what adults call 'easier' feeding. When this happens, meals can take on the appearance of a factory conveyor belt, and do not become the social times that they should be. If anyone was invited round for a meal, they would be horrified if they were seated in a line, so why should babies be any different? Chairs should be placed in a semi-circle style so that the babies can talk to one another and make eye contact. The adult should place herself on a chair at the same level as the babies, not kneeling on the floor or bending over them to put food into their mouths. Meal times should be a source of social inter-action and learning, not a time to be 'got through'. Many high chairs are inappropriate for use in day care settings, where all of the tables are child height. The traditional high chair was designed to bring the baby to the same height as an adult-sized table in a home; as a conse-quence, the adults who feed babies in traditional high chairs are standing over them or kneeling on the floor to feed them. Neither situation is ideal.

As well as giving babies the right place to sleep, it is also important that nurseries have enough floor space to enable babies to be offered some tummy time. Since the introduction of the 'Back to Sleep' campaign to reduce the incidence of SIDS (Sudden Infant Death Syndrome), many parents and practitioners are loathe to place their babies on their tummies, but neonatal physiotherapist Peta Smith says:

> By spending time on their tummies babies learn to move from side to side and this helps them learn to reach and crawl. Not only does tummy time help with coordination, balance and postural control, which is the foundation for all movement skills, it increases babies' confidence and independence helping them to become motivated to explore their surroundings as they learn to control their bodies. (Smith, 2006)

Many parents and practitioners say that babies do not like to be placed on their tummies but this can be achieved in many ways such as laying a baby across the knee or laying them on your chest or, as observed in a day nursery, by placing yourself on your front facing the baby. This observation was particularly good because the baby was interacting with the adult and making good eye contact, as well as raising her head to look around the room thus strengthening her muscles.

When looking at the floor in baby rooms, it is important to pay attention to the floor covering. Many homes and care settings favour the use of laminate flooring, but this can be a problem for emergent walkers. These floors are fabulous for crawling because the baby can go at speed but when a baby is beginning to pull themselves up and when they are taking their first steps, it can be very difficult thus making the baby or toddler less confident in their mobility skills. It is also important in baby rooms to give the babies and toddlers the opportunity to walk on different surfaces; the world outside is not completely flat, and so early walkers need the experience of moving from one surface level to another.

One possible ideal layout for a room is to have a kitchen area with sink, tables etc., where the babies can engage in messy play and where they eat their meals. This area could then lead into a room that was reminiscent of a front room, one carpeted with soft furnishings and curtains. With a low window for babies to look into the garden, the room would have large amounts of natural light. Leading on from this, there could be a changing area and another area for a bedroom where the babies could be put to sleep in their cots.

Many nurseries put babies outside to sleep, but some settings encounter parents who do not want their babies to be put outside. In fact, when this was mentioned to a father with a new baby, he was horrified, as are some practitioners when this is discussed at training sessions. Again, when looking into their reasons for this, it all comes down to safety, but with thought most nursery and home gardens can be made secure to ensure a baby's physical safety. More nurseries need to engage in this practice, as they have a duty to ensure that these babies are given access to fresh air on a daily basis.

Outdoor spaces and access

Looking at access to an outdoor environment is another important factor for parents to consider when looking at a nursery. One of the most important statutory requirements of the EYFS (DfES, 2007) states that:

> Children must have opportunities to play indoors and outdoors. All early years providers must have access to an outdoor play area which can benefit the children. If a setting does not have direct access to an outdoor play area then they must make arrangements for daily opportunities for outdoor play in an appropriate nearby location. (DfES, 2007, Practice Guidance, p. 7)

The city-based nursery that took part in my research did not have any access to an outdoor environment, which had an impact on what opportunities they could offer to the children. They did take the children out in their buggies or to walk to the shops but this did not meet all of the needs of all of the children, as illustrated by my reflections below on Martin's and Georgina's experiences which appear less positive because they had no access to an outdoor environment, something which would have supported their learning styles.

 Case study 15

One of the areas of weakness in this setting which evolved during the case study narrative of these three children was the lack of or limited access to an outdoor environment. I felt that two of the children, Georgina and Martin, did not have their needs met because there was no outdoor area which the children could explore or access independently. The staff in the setting did try to take the children out on a daily basis, but this was by necessity adult-directed. Unlike the vision of the McMillan sisters (McMillan, 1930), these children did not have the opportunity to engage with an area which could challenge their gross motor development or expose them to outdoor exploratory or sensory experiences.

As in the case of the day nursery which took part in my research, many nurseries and pre-schools have issues about being able to access the outside on a daily basis. In some authorities, very few of the nurseries have baby or very young children's rooms upstairs, but even when they are on the ground floor adults often do not see it as a necessity for these very young children to access the outside other than at what feels like 'playtime'. When the younger babies and children are placed upstairs, this is because the adults see this as a right for the older children to access this outdoor environment. Why should this be? Is it because it is easier to open the doors and to let the older children 'free-flow' between the indoors and outdoors? Where are the rights of the very young children to this access?

One day nursery has worked through this dilemma by building some decking and a canopy outside the baby room, which is separate from the main play area and the nursery does not just see this as an opportunity to be utilized in the summer months. The nursery accesses this area in all weathers, with very young children sitting on rugs in their hats and coats playing with the heuristic, open-ended resources which children can explore and use as they want (Goldschmied and Jackson, 2004) or accessing a range of age-appropriate gross motor equipment. Heuristic play resources are not items which can be purchased from toy shops, they are resources which can be used in a variety of ways, needing no instruction as to their use or purpose from the adults. This is quality practice and is what every child, irrespective of age, should have access to.

Another problem with accessing the outdoor environment is the allocation of a 'shift' pattern when it comes to going outside. When this practice is questioned, the response is often centered around concerns about health and safety issues, the younger children's safety evidently compromised by the presence of the older, more robust children. But is this the case? In Case study 16, we can see how the older children have free-flow access to the outdoor environment all day, while the younger children access this environment as and when they want to. All of the children, irrespective of age, have been accessing the outdoors at the same time. This is a large nursery, situated in a domestic house, with all the restrictions that this entails, and yet all of the children can be outside safely. There is a large range of gross motor equipment that enables children of differing ages and capabilities to have appropriate access, and a range of adult-planned and child-initiated activity. This nursery has invested in staffing; the adults in this nursery support the children, interacting with them as appropriate and not going into super-vision mode, which can frequently happen when adults go outside. Here, all the children have the right to be outside.

   Case study 16

All of the children have gone outside. It is a sunny day and the garden is well shaded by mature trees overhanging the garden space. There is a range of climbing and balancing equipment which offers challenge to children of differing ages. There is a rug under one of the trees for non-mobile babies to sit and share books with adults. One baby who is just beginning to walk crawls off the mat towards the fence where there are some hanging mobiles and wind chimes. He sits playing with these for a while before crawling to the balancing apparatus. He pulls himself up and, using the equipment as a support, walks alongside holding on. When he reaches the end, he then crawls off towards the top end of the garden which is full of plants and flowers. He crawls around this area before finding a push-along toy which he then uses to guide himself back to the rug.

This expedition took him nearly half an hour but what impressed me was the way in which he was free to explore and also the way in which when he sat back he could sit and watch all of the other older children accessing the different areas. At no time was he in danger and although he was on his own, he was being observed all the time by the adults.

It is when discussing access to an outdoor environment that the childminder can have a distinct advantage over other types of day care provider. Like mothers who stay at home to bring up their children, the childminder can access the outdoor environment and the local community at all times of the day. Frequently, the childminder is walking to and from school to drop off and pick up older children, she is going to the shops and the library and she is visiting local parks. An example of quality practice is the childminder who accesses different parks according to the ages of the children that she has on that day; she ensures that each child is able to access a play environment which offers the children physical challenge appropriate to their age and stage of development.

Lighting

Another environmental issue which needs addressing is the use of lighting. How many of us, especially in the winter months, turn on the light at the beginning of the day and never bother to turn it off until we leave at the end of the day? How many of us who spend a lot of our time in offices, in rooms with strip or powerful lighting, go home at the end of the day with tired eyes and frequently with a headache? Natural light in an environment is important, and many nurseries do not bear this in mind when they paint murals over the windows. This practice in essence cuts down on the light that enters the rooms and often serves no other purpose than advertising. Why do we need paintings of butterflies and rainbows on the windows? We do not do this in our own homes. In some nurseries, they are conscious of the lighting, and do have periods of the day when they use lower-level or no lighting. The lower-level lighting is achieved through the use of battery-operated fairy lights and small LED lights. It appears that when nurseries employ this practice, the room becomes calmer and there can be an improved level of behaviour as a result. Another practical point about lighting which needs to be considered when the room is being designed is to have some lights on different relays or switches, thus allowing the practitioners the opportunity of making one area of the room darker than another. This is of particular use in a room where some of the children go to sleep and others do not.

When reflecting on physical environments for babies and toddlers, I think my biggest wish would be for all of these rooms to be quiet, calm and reflective places, as opposed to the sometimes bright over-stimulating rooms that are encountered in some day nurseries. As we will see in the next chapter, young children respond to experiences through their senses, and some of the highest levels of involvement and wellbeing are visible when they are engaged with natural, open-ended and heuristic resources.

Colours

When looking at creating an environment for babies, practitioners need to be aware of how to present one which is calm and not over-stimulating. Traditionally, society has provided young children with vibrant, primary-coloured resources and décor. The work of Elizabeth Jarman on Communication Friendly Spaces (2009) advocates using neutral wall colours, supported by resources which are naturalistic and tactile.

Colours can also be used to stimulate very young babies. Murray and Andrews in *The Social Baby* (2000) use high-contrast black and white images close to a baby's limited focal distance.

 Case study 17: Oscar at under 2 months old

At a very early age, Oscar is seen to be looking around his environment. His ability to focus is limited, and so his mother decides to put a black and white image in his Moses basket within his focal distance. He immediately locks on to the image and maintains his attention on the area that is black and white. In his few moments of interaction with the world around him, he is beginning to show levels of involvement and concentration. This interest in the high contrast colours is also evident when his grandmother is wearing a black and white dress which he looks at intently.

This case study illustrates how a very young baby is interested in high contrast areas. Although babies who access day care settings are older than this, many settings have now established black and white areas.

 Questions for reflection

- How do you ensure that the transition from room to room is not traumatic for babies and young children and parents? Are parents involved in the same way in the 'new room' as they were when their child first started at the nursery?

- Why it is important to group children according to their age, and why are many practitioners adverse to mixed-age rooms?
- What do you think of moving babies and children as a group, to enable friendships to support transition?

Further reading

Jarman, E. (2009) *The Communication Friendly Spaces Approach*. Kent: Elizabeth Jarman Ltd.

This toolkit provides 20 case studies to encourage practitioners to reflect on the learning environment as a means of developing speaking and listening skills.

References

David, T., Goouch, K., Powell, S. and Abbott, L. (2003) *Birth to Three Matters: A Review of the Literature*. Nottingham: DfES Publications.

Department for Education and Skills (DfES) (2007) *Statutory Framework for the Early Years Foundation Stage: Setting the Standards for Learning, Development and Care for Children from Birth to Five*. Nottingham: DfES Publications.

Goldschmied, E. and Jackson, S. (2004) *People Under Three: Young Children in Day Care*, 2nd edn. London: Routledge.

Jarman, E. (2009) *The Communication Friendly Spaces Approach*. Kent: Elizabeth Jarman Ltd.

McMillan, M. (1930) *The Nursery School* (Revised edition). London: J.M. Dent & Sons: E.P. Dutton.

Mathers, S. and Sylva, K. (2007) *National Evaluation of the Neighbourhood Nurseries Initiative: The Relationship between Quality and Children's Behavioural Development*. Nottingham: DfES Publications.

Mathers, S., Sylva, K. and Joshi, H. (2007) *The Quality of Childcare Settings in the Millennium Cohort Study*. Nottingham: DfES Publications.

Murray, L. and Andrews, L. (2000) *The Social Baby*. Richmond: CP Publishing.

Smith, P. (2006) quoted in Elliott, J. 'Babies need "tummy time" to develop,' *The Guardian*, 1 July. Available at http://news.bbc.co.uk/1/hi/5128144.stm

The Scottish Government (2010) *Pre-Birth to Three: Positive Outcomes for Scotland's Children and Families*. Edinburgh: Scottish Government.

Vygotsky, L. (1978) *Mind in Society: The Development of Higher Psychological Processes*. London: Harvard University Press.

Useful websites

http://corporate.csp.midev.rroom.net/director/newsandevents/physio
   alerts.cfm?item id=FC7D80659A0C002D7266B79FE9339550
www.elizabethjarmantraining.co.uk/
www.ltscotland.org.uk/earlyyears/prebirthtothree/index.asp

5 The Creative Environment

This chapter will:

- explain the complexity of the creative environment and the role of the adult in planning directed activities
- highlight the value of babies and young children experiencing learning through their senses
- present some examples of how to use the creative environment through treasure basket, heuristic and exploratory play
- discuss children's early schematic play.

When thinking of a creative environment for babies and young children, we have to think of an environment where it is possible for children to express their originality through using their imaginations, exploring, taking risks and having fun. Perhaps it is because of the abstract nature of creativity that many environments and activities for babies and young children can lack inspiration. The complexity of creativity is recognized in the EYFS Practice Guidance (DfES, 2007).

One of the problems with creativity is agreeing on what this means. The EYFS Practice Guidance describes creativity for young children in the following manner:

- Creativity is about taking risks and making connections and is strongly linked to play.
- Creativity emerges as children become absorbed in action and explorations of their own ideas, expressing them through movement, making and transforming things using media and materials such as crayons, paints, scissors, words, sounds, movement, props and make-believe.

- Creativity involves children in initiating their own learning and making choices and decisions.
- Children's responses to what they see, hear and experience through their senses are individual and the way they represent their experiences is unique and valuable.
- Being creative enables babies and children to explore many processes, media and materials and to make new things emerge as a result. (DfES, 2007, p. 106)

A further definition of creativity can be found in the National Advisory Committee on Creative and Cultural Education (NACCCE) report (1999), *All Our Futures: Creativity, Culture and Education,* when it states that creativity is: 'imaginative activity fashioned so as to produce outcomes that are both original and of value.' This definition is relevant as it illustrates how babies and young children should be given opportunities to engage and experience with their senses so that they can make links and interpret in their own way; it is only by letting them be free to ponder and muse that they will become the critical and creative thinkers of the future.

Reggio Emilia is the epitome of creativity in education. This town in Italy has created a programme for children in the early years to explore, experience and investigate through their creativity. This programme does not talk about children's artistic abilities but about how children develop holistically. At the core of the programme is the experienced teacher who 'listens' to the children and involves them at the centre of decision making. 'Listening means being fully attentive to the children, and at the same time, taking responsibility for recording and documenting what is observed and then using it as a basis for decision making shared with children and parents' (Edwards et al., 1998). Although this programme would not be totally transferable to other countries' early years programmes, as it is unique to the town where it was developed, it has an ethos and philosophy that any practitioner working in the early years will benefit from listening to, especially in their attitude to and understanding of what creativity is.

Adult-directed activities

In settings, creativity is often seen as young children producing a product as evidence to parents that they have been doing something worthwhile whilst they have been in nursery. There are many discussions with practitioners talking about the status of 'craft' work being the sole evidence of learning. Practitioners could use the example of children playing in the water tray, experimenting and exploring its properties. Here, learning is taking place, but obviously no practitioner could divide up the water and send this home as evidence of learning. Varied ways of communicating what can constitute creative activity need to be found.

When practitioners care for babies and young children in out-of-home settings, they have to realize that they are not a 'craft' factory and that children need to be given the space and opportunity to express themselves creatively in a wide range of ways. This expression is not about giving babies and children pre-drawn pictures for them to colour in; this is the adult's interpretation and not the child's. Over the number of years that I have worked with practitioners, I have seen many products which have been 'created' by babies; these are in fact a tribute to the artistic talent of the practitioner and have nothing to do with the baby. We still frequently see adults painting babies and young children's hands, and then pressing them onto paper. This is a lovely memento for parents, but often children will choose to do this on their own if the resources and opportunities are made available to them. The following case study is of an observation of some children aged between 2 and 2½ years of age demonstrating just this.

 Case study 18: Lynda at 2 years 4 months old

- Lynda goes over to the painting easel and puts on an apron without any adult assistance. She stands in front of the easel; there is nothing to paint with and no paper. She brushes her hands over the smooth surface of the easel.
- The adult sees this and responds and asks her if she wants some paper. Lynda is offered a choice and she selects pink. The paper is clipped up and Lynda says, 'Painting. I got an apron on'.
- Lynda is not perturbed by having to wait. At one time, the adult suggests that she goes to paint with another adult who is about to do a painting activity. Lynda does not respond so the adult goes off to find Lynda some paint.
- As she gets the paints, Lynda says the names of the colours and begins to paint with a brush and then she begins to use her hands to mix the paint that is on the paper. When she is doing this, Lynda makes lots of 'Oh' noises. Lynda now starts to take the paint out of the pots with her hands to put onto the paper.

(Continued)

(Continued)

- Lynda is not at all bothered when some other children are attracted to what she is doing and start to join in with her picture by putting their hands on the wet paint. More and more children come over to join in with her. One boy in particular persists in putting paint on his hands from Lynda's picture.
- Lynda is getting very excited and she tells the others that the painting is becoming unattached: 'It's coming off! Wait' – she tries to put it back on herself. She talks to the others: 'Don't rip paper. I painting on it.' The paper falls off: 'My picture', she keeps repeating to protect her painting from another boy taking it. Lynda is assertive but not aggressive.
- As the paper falls down, Lynda starts to paint the surface of the easel.
- As the boy who was getting his hands in the paint has been putting prints all over the room and the furniture, the adult has responded to this by putting large pieces of paper on the wall with some paint by the side.
- The adult asks Lynda if she would like to come and join in with this activity and put her hands on the wall. Lynda goes over to join in.
- Lynda turns round to show everyone her paint-covered hands.

This whole activity followed the interests of Lynda and the boy, as well as those of the other children. The boy's handprints all over the room were perfect; he did not need an adult to paint his hand and then hold it down. This episode illustrates how children's creativity can be extended by an understanding adult following the children's needs and interests. In all of the observations of Lynda, it was clear that she enjoyed exploring with her hands in an independent manner and this case study illustrates how, with the support of the adult, she is able to develop this creativity as well as her social interaction, which was an area of Lynda's development that needed extending, as is evident from the following observations of Lynda in the following two months.

 Lynda at 2 years 5 months old

- Lynda is now putting her hands on the paper but she seems just to put the prints in the same place. When the adult suggests that she stand so that she can reach across the paper, Lynda does so. She keeps saying 'Tickle, tickle'.
- When she is doing the printing, she keeps looking to the adult for comment.
- 'Can I have more paint?'

(Continued)

- The adult comments that Lynda is doing the printing quickly and, in response, Lynda gets even quicker. She is enjoying spreading the paint over the paper – not just making prints.

 Lynda at 2 years 6 months old

- When she feels the paint, she says that it tickles.
- Lynda starts to imitate the shape mark making in the paint by the adult, using her finger to make the shape marks in the wet paint.
- Lynda gets down from the table to wash her hands.
- She soon returns to her painting.
- She talks to me, telling me that she's painting and again she asks for more paint. She is animated in her expressions and she asks the adult to hold the tray for her while she rubs her hands in the paint on the tray.

Treasure baskets and heuristic play

When babies are very young, they need to be exposed to experiences so that they can make connections in their learning. The way in which babies learn is through exploration using their senses. In recent times, many practitioners have looked to the work of Elinor Goldschmied (2004) to offer babies these experiences through play with treasure baskets. It has become almost a fad and can be used inappropriately if we forget the fundamental principles of offering babies this type of sensory experience. Goldschmied and Jackson (2004) state that the treasure basket '… gathers together and provides a focus for a rich variety of everyday objects chosen to offer stimulus to these different senses'. Young babies who can sit but have still yet to master the necessary motor coordination to crawl or walk can be extremely frustrated, as they cannot reach the things they want for themselves. The treasure basket gives them autonomy in their play, something which they find difficult to replicate in other areas of their life. The treasure basket offers them choice and the opportunity to explore and investigate materials which are open-ended; again passing the decision making as to how to use these resources back to them. Frequently, practitioners do not give babies this autonomous opportunity; they feel the need to show a baby how to use the resource, and because they feel that they are not supporting the babies unless they are interacting, they intervene and frequently take this play over. This is a strange situation; often practitioners talk about the difficulty in finding the time to do observations of babies and yet treasure basket play, if it is done properly, gives them the perfect opportunity to sit back and watch what the babies decide to do with the resources that have been offered to them. This type of play will show what materials the babies are interested in, what their preferred learning styles are and what their levels of concentration and involvement are. It will also suggest ideas for how adults can offer babies future activities away from the treasure basket which will help to challenge the play of these very young children.

The treasure basket play case study of Sam in Chapter 2 demonstrates the power of this play. In the case study, Sam is showing how he uses the resources to be creative; he is not producing a product but he is learning through his senses, thus having the opportunity to feel texture, make sounds, explore the properties of different objects and use the senses in his mouth to make links with all of those experiences.

When practitioners are using the treasure basket play, they need to go back to the 'rules' described by Goldschmied and Jackson (2004) as follows:

- This type of play is for non-mobile babies.
- The basket needs to evolve and change constantly.
- Items in the basket are to be clean.
- The play is only for use with a maximum of three babies.
- Babies should be seated at an angle to the basket.
- Adults must not intervene but should stay quiet and attentive.
- It should be ensured that mobile babies do not disturb the play.
  (Adapted from Goldschmied and Jackson, 2004)

When working with parents or childminders, there is always a difficulty firstly in obtaining a basket, at a reasonable price, that adheres to Goldschmied and Jackson's recommendations. I think when discussing with parents of young babies how to use a treasure basket at home, it is important to remember that shopping around for these resources is not always necessary. The baskets are meant to be filled with everyday objects that are readily found in the home. If, however, parents want to buy the resources to keep them in the basket, I conducted an experiment of going to three high-street supermarkets located in my area to see what resources I could buy cheaply that would be appropriate for a treasure basket whilst I was doing my weekly shop. It was an interesting experiment and the results are as shown below. The main difficulty was in sourcing a proper basket, and I am afraid that on this occasion I decided not to be purist as I felt that it was important to get parents to look at offering their babies these experiences.

Supermarket 1	Balloon whisk	£0.99
	Flat whisk	£0.99
	Tea strainer	£0.79
	Pastry brush	£0.99
	Jigger	£1.99
Supermarket 2	Metal egg cup	£0.60
	2x wooden spoons & 1 spatula	£1.25
	Bought as a set:	
	Nail brush	£4.09
	Loofah	
	Pumice stone	
	Back strap	
	Covered sponge	
Supermarket 3	Bowl	£0.50
	Wooden lemon squeezer	£0.97
	Basket	£5.00
	Honey drizzler	£0.99
	Dish mop	£0.99
TOTAL		£20.17

Figure 5.1   A supermarket treasure basket

All of the items in this treasure basket were bought from the local supermarket. Other items were found in the home.

I have become known as the odd woman who gives a present of a basket of wood when babies are born, but despite the initial mocking, parents always come back and tell me that the treasure basket has become one of their child's favourite toys.

As this book is looking at learning environments, it is also relevant to look at heuristic play for young children and toddlers. As Goldschmied and Jackson (2004) recognize: 'Children in their second year feel a great urge to explore and discover for themselves the way objects behave in space as they manipulate them.' Heuristic play is a way of building on the levels of concentration and involvement that young babies experienced with the treasure basket. This is play that has to be agreed on by a whole staff team and where there is sufficient space and time to enable the children to explore the open-ended resources in a discrete session.

An example of how young children can use open-ended resources in their own way would be when I become involved in the play of a young child who was 14 months old. She came to sit near me and there was a tin of chocolates with empty sweet papers in it. These wrappers were shiny and crinkly so she was offered the tin; she crawled behind the chairs and started to play with the papers, putting them in and out of the box, scrunching them in her fingers and looking at them. She became completely absorbed. The adult role in this was to sit, watch and be fascinated as she played for over half an hour. The light bulb moment came when another adult passed the scene and exclaimed, 'Look at that, she doesn't need fancy toys'. This is a comment that adults make every Christmas and birthday, and yet we still persist on providing toys for children that are plastic, brightly coloured, expensive and 'all singing and dancing'.

Holland (1997) used the principles of heuristic play when she described the exploratory play sessions that she established within her setting. These sessions are for young children to be able to explore the properties of materials such as glue. In her case study, Holland demonstrates that very young children can become involved, challenged and show high levels of concentration if the conditions are right. Like Goldschmied, Holland makes the exploratory sessions discrete with no adult involvement and without any interruption of noise or external stimulus.

I frequently see young children being offered glue and then 'encouraged' to stick pieces of material or paper onto 'their picture'. If the practitioners took a step back and really observed the children with the glue, they would see that the children want to explore the glue to see what it will do. Does it drizzle? What pattern can I make? Why does it do that? Why are my hands dry? Can I peel this stuff off my hands? All of these questions can be seen formulating in the young child's mind, so why do we as adults feel obliged to take this over with our agendas so that what the child is doing represents something? This is about the young child thinking about and planning what they can do with materials. These are skills that will help these young children in their learning as they progress through the education system. The following case study demonstrates how Amy wants to make her own decisions about how to use the glue and when she has had enough.

    Case study 19: Amy at 2 years 1 month old

When I go into the room, Amy is standing at the table watching a few children doing a gluing activity with the adult.

- Amy asks the adult if she can do a picture.
- The adult tells her to go and get a chair so that she can sit down – Amy follows these instructions.

- Another child starts to get on her chair and Amy says, 'That's my chair' and sits down.
- Amy starts to glue and she is laughing.
- Amy is concentrating – she is really involved in what she is doing.
- When the adult offers Amy paper to stick on as the other children are doing, Amy makes it clear that this is not what she wants to do – she is interested in the glue that is her picture. She also shows that she doesn't like the way in which the paper gets stuck to her glue stick or to her fingers.
- During this activity, Amy is very relaxed and at ease. She is very precise in her movements. She knows exactly what she wants to do – she is not easily distracted and, if she does look up, it is only momentarily.
- Amy uses the glue stick to dig the last remains of glue from the bottom of the pot. The adult suggests that they will have to clear away for snack time – Amy says, 'Not finished yet!' – I was pleased that the adult accepted this and did not interrupt Amy's activity. Amy's speech is clear and distinct.
- As she is using the glue stick, she is using up and down movements. She uses the stick to mix in the pot.
- Amy also initiates conversation with adults as well as other children.
- Amy has sustained this play/activity for three quarters of an hour with real concentration. She now looks over to the ball pool and says, 'I've finished now'.

This case study clearly shows how Amy is using the glue in her own way, following her own agenda and, as a result, showing high levels of involvement.

Experiencing creativity

For me, some of the most memorable observations of practice have been when practitioners have stripped babies down to their nappies so that they can really get involved with paint; not with a paint brush but through moving their hands in the paint and then finding out what it feels like when it is on their bodies. This is pure creativity by the babies. Adults worry about the mess but, after this exploration of paint, the babies and adults can explore water through water play – and give the babies a bath.

One such observation was experienced recently when a 2-year-old child was sitting on the floor with a range of paint colours and a variety of tools to express herself as she wanted to on a very large piece of paper. After having experimented with the brushes and spatulas, she began to squeeze the paint off the brushes and through her hands. She rubbed the paint into her hands before deciding that she wanted to put these onto the paper – a perfect handprint! She then moved onto another colour. This involvement went on for over 40 minutes without interruption from the adults; all the other children had moved away from the activity but she was allowed to persevere until she had finished exploring the paint. This observation also revealed the skills of the practitioner who recognized the child's need and desire to investigate the paint for herself and to experiment with it.

Schemas

This child was exploring and expressing her own creativity but perhaps her behaviour was something completely different. Was the covering of her hands with paint an example of a schema, a pattern of repeatable behaviour within play? As the work of Athey (2006) and Nutbrown (2011) demonstrates, young children's learning can be linked to their schema. In this case, is the child demonstrating an enclosing behaviour as she covers her hands with paint, enclosing her hands? Probably, yes as earlier this child told me that the shell goes *inside* when playing with the horse chestnut cases and conkers in the interactive autumn display.

The following case study illustrates one child's schematic play as observed by his mother. Luke is demonstrating his creativity through an enclosing schema. From his mother's description, it is clear that Luke's schematic play is extended when his parents key in to his play and enable him to explore and experiment through his chosen pattern of behaviour.

 Case study 20: Luke

From about I year of age onwards, Luke demonstrated schematic play in unlikely situations. He climbed into a toy box and sat inside to read a book and play. Shortly after his first birthday, whilst playing in the garden, he climbed into an unfeasibly small plastic bowl filled with water and sat contentedly, apparently exploring the feeling of being in a tight enclosed space. He would also bury himself under towels, blankets and duvets.

When we bought a new vacuum cleaner, he hid inside the box. It seemed important for him to close the lid on top of himself each time, before emerging to repeat the play.

At 18 months, he combined this enveloping and enclosing behaviour with a different schema – lining up objects. He had a set of cutlery with hollow handles, which he stacked up vertically, one inside the other.

At 2 years 7 months, Luke rearranged the nativity scene, lining up the figures horizontally along the window sill. He said it was a traffic jam. Concurrent with this, he continued to demonstrate his preferred schema of covering things up. On one occasion, he painted an entire broadsheet newspaper with orange paint, before moving on to paint the length of his left arm, all the time describing his actions. A month later, he enjoyed the wintry weather, carefully digging and piling snow on top of a toy train until it was completely hidden.

When he was 2 years 9 months, Luke spent 30 minutes or more rolling out play dough, flattening it and wrapping up three of his favourite toy engines individually, before lining them up along the track. He used shredded paper and two strings of sparkly Christmas beads to cover up trains on his track. By this stage, some of the play was accompanied by contextual explanations. On this occasion, his narration revealed that the paper and beads represented snow and ice on the track; he was re-enacting part of a story he had enjoyed at the time.

Luke is now 4 years old and these schemas are sometimes in evidence, but less often. We bought another vacuum cleaner last week and, once again, he chose to get inside the box and close the lid on top of himself. This time though, the play was related to being a pirate and the box represented his ship, in contrast to his former need to enclose himself for its own sake.

I have worked with staff in several settings who have used their observations to identify children's different schema, and to use these observations to lead their planning. In order to do this, all of the adults have to have a good knowledge of the different schema, as well as the opportunity for teams to discuss individual children, so that the environment and resources can be adapted to enable children to explore and learn through their identified schema.

Creativity through music

One aspect of creativity which many practitioners often shy away from is music. They are perfectly happy to sing rhymes with the children, but can feel either self-conscious or not skilled enough when offering young children the opportunity to experiment with instruments to create sounds. One of the issues with musical instruments is that children can quite often create a cacophony of sound which can disturb other children or dominate the talking space within a room. What adults need to be aware of when offering children this type of play is where they place the instruments and how they support the children in their exploration of music. The following case study demonstrates how the adults have chosen an appropriate space to offer one young child this experience. This observation lasted for half an hour and showed not only the value of the opportunity to engage with creating music, but also the opportunity for social development; this was quite important in this case as this child's mother had placed her son in day care for the express reason of social development.

 Case study 21: Josh at 2 years 6 months old

Josh is quite a sensitive child and if I've been with friends and there's been lots of children around, he has cried a lot and like he's shy and he doesn't like a lot of social situations or it takes him a long time. (Mother of Josh)

- Josh makes some noises with the instruments and asks, 'What was that?' and replies, 'I think it might be me'.
- Josh then says, 'What's this?' I reply that it is a xylophone. Josh then continues to play on the other instruments. He echoes some of the musical sounds that I make. He then notices that the xylophone has numbers 1–8 on the keys. He recognizes these numbers in order and in isolation and knows that certain numbers come before or after.
- As he plays on the instruments, Josh spontaneously starts to sing Old McDonald had a Farm. Another boy comes over and starts to sing Baa, Baa Black Sheep, but Josh reverts back to his own tune. Josh is not concerned that another child has joined us but he is sure enough of himself to continue as he wants to. He carries on playing, telling me that he is playing me a tune. He tells me to watch as he drags the stick over the keys on the xylophone. He then tells me to watch again as he uses different sticks to produce different sounds on the different instruments.
- One of the instruments has a hole in the end and Josh tells me that the stick goes into this hole. He also tells me that the other children in the room are reading books.

- Josh begins to sing again and, as before, he keeps returning to Old McDonald even though different children try to change the tune to something else.
- Josh doesn't play with the children directly – it is parallel play but he is quite content for them to be near him and to be in his space. Also, although he was the only one playing with the instruments at the start, he doesn't get frustrated when the others join in and he is quite happy for them to use the instruments.
- Josh then moves away to sit on a chair and continues with his movement from the music session by bouncing up and down on the chair.

Looking back at the first observations and the comments made by his mother as to her reasons for putting Josh into nursery, in order to develop his social skills, I would say that this objective has been achieved; he is safe and secure in his environment and he is not disturbed when other children invade his space.

Interestingly, I think the challenge for Josh now is for the adults in the room to give him appropriate challenge. I have noticed over the past two observations that Josh is interested and enjoys engaging with the musical instruments, and yet I don't think the adults have used this interest to extend his learning. Josh is very popular with the adults in the room and they are fascinated by his language and are aware of his abilities, but they don't see the need to move this forward. I would suggest that the majority of Josh's language and learning has come from home. I think that this is evident in the way in which he approaches reading, and the way in which he handles books. From the evidence of the other children and from the way in which the adults interact, I would suggest that this is not taking place in the nursery.

Representational or role play

As discussed earlier on in this chapter, children do not always have to produce something for them to be creative. What they need is the opportunity to explore and experiment. Young children's very early experiences come from the home and in their role play they use their observations from this environment and play them out. In settings, it is often found that the resources for this type of play for very young children are too sophisticated and complicated and, as a result, the adults get frustrated when the children do not play 'properly' with the resources. Children of this age do not need complicated kitchen units and fancy dressing-up clothes to get into role. Look at what children of this age like doing: they like putting things in bags, often a sign of schematic play; they like 'going to the shops'; they like using pots and pans, real ones; and they love looking at themselves in mirrors dressed up in hats and shoes, depending on their age. Some of the role-play clothes that we have are too complicated to put on independently or easily and are sometimes representative of roles of which very young children have no experience and therefore cannot relate to. Do under 2s really understand the roles of paramedics, policemen or firemen? The following case study shows just how one boy engages in some creative role play in the bathroom at a nursery. What he is thinking of we can only speculate, but there is purpose to his play and he sustains it for as long as it is safe for him to do so.

 Case study 22: Tim at 2 years 5 months old

- The activity on offer is not a challenging activity and so Tim concentrates and remains interested for only a few moments. There is concentration whilst he is doing the painting. He goes to wash his hands.
- The adult makes a comment to me to explain that Tim likes running water and that he still has a close relationship with Amy but that he now likes to join in with the boisterous play of the other boys.
- Tim is still in the bathroom washing his hands so I position myself so that I can see what he is doing. He is soaping/washing the mirrors and then wiping them. He tells me what he is doing. He squeezes the water out of the cloth (paper towel) – in this activity, he is completely absorbed and interested – there is real concentration. There is a purpose to what he is doing. He then pretends to lick the cloth to wipe the mirrors. He sustains this activity for at least 10 minutes – he washes his face and becomes more and more interested in the water and then in washing the floor where some of the water has spilled. The adult has to call him out as the floor is getting wet and this poses a risk – I was pleased that the adult let him sustain this interest of his until it became unsafe.

Role play for young children can be seen in their play with small-world resources. It is always fascinating to watch the storytelling that young children who are not yet vocalizing can be seen to be doing when they are engaging with the small world. You frequently see their lips moving or notice that they are moving the resources about in a purposeful and meaningful way. The following case study demonstrates the power of James' storytelling as he engages with the cars on the table and then extends this storytelling into his mark making and then into his social interaction with me.

Case study 23: James at 2 years 7 months old

- James goes over to where the small world is set up on a table. He goes to get a chair to bring to the table.
- James is concentrating on his play but he does occasionally look up to see what is going on in the rest of the room.
- As he plays with his small world, James is talking to himself – he is telling a story as he moves the cars etc. around. I can't decipher the words and do not want to get closer because I might disrupt his play.
- As he is telling the story, James laughs out loud.
- Although he is quite happy for others to be on the table as well, he does not want anyone near him to disturb his play – he is still solitary playing. When he finds a car on another table, he is still claiming possession – 'MINE'.
- James leaves the room to go to the toilet
- He comes over to the mark making and says that he is doing a racing car – he says that he can't do it.
- We talk about the wheels on cars and he goes to draw the wheels.
- He then moves off and is carrying a basket. I ask him to go and do the shopping for me.
- He returns with it and then goes back into the role-play area. He is very busy and occupied.
- He is role playing on his own but again this is a high level of play.
- He returns to me for the basket and begins to tell what he has got in it.

When I next visited the setting, the adult told me of some play she had observed between James and another girl. It was small-world play again but this time he was involved with another child.

Role play can also be across the many facets of creativity. Today many young children are exposed to performance competitions; programmes like *The X Factor* and *Britain's Got Talent* in the UK dominate our television screens. This means that when visiting nurseries, you often see very young children 'performing', displaying their self-confidence as they demonstrate how they can sing and dance. I saw an excellent example of this when visiting a day nursery. The 2-year-olds were outside and in one corner of this area there is a stage with some small seats for an audience. One young child was availing herself of the open-ended dressing-up props that the adults had placed next to this area. These props were not manufactured costumes for the children to dress up in, but articles and materials which could be many things according to the interpretation of the individual child. For example, an old curtain can be a Superhero's cloak to one child, to another it can be the cloak of a princess, and to yet another it can be the means by which to create a den, which in turn can be a cave, a bedroom or anything that the child wants. These resources can be starting points of a child's creative thinking. The young girl had a length of fabric over her shoulders as she arranged her 'audience'. She then began her performance. This observation showed how very young children can display their creativity using their experiences from home to demonstrate their individual talents.

Creativity through technology

Today babies and young children are exposed to modern technology at a very early age. They frequently use this technology in their representational play as they get hold of the remote control and point it at the television or pick up a Lego brick and use it as a telephone. Many of the commercial toys bought for children today are interactive and replace some of the child's own creativity. If a child presses a button, he will produce a sound, so why does he need to be exposed to musical instruments? This does not mean to say that the use of such cause-and-effect resources is detrimental to a child's creative development. The following case study tracks Sam's use of technology over a period of three years and how he puts this to use in developing skills in other areas of learning.

  Case study 24: Sam

When Sam is 11 months old, Rachel, his mother, makes the following observation:
    He plays with the pop toys for quite a while. He likes to push things. He has now got his own remote control because he broke it so we had to buy Liam a new one and put it out of reach. When Liam is playing, he absolutely loves to sit next to Liam just doing the buttons – which is outrageous to think an 11-month-old is able to manipulate a Game Boy. He investigates all of the buttons. If Liam is doing it, that is what he will choose to do, to get this out. Now he has his own, it is better because he was always fighting, trying to get it off Liam. Now he has this, he will sit next to Liam and it looks like he is really playing it.
    When Sam is 14 months old, he becomes fascinated by my camera and tape recorder:
    Sam comes over to me as I am using the camera. He has a piece of paper and starts to write on it. Rachel comments that he likes the camera. She gets his camera out and they start to press the buttons which then has a response – he

obviously enjoys cause-and-effect resources. Rachel notices that as he uses his thumb he is only using his left hand, as if the thumb is stronger on that hand and he can't do the same action with his other hand. He crawls over to me and starts to investigate the tape recorder; he can see something turning round and then spends a long time trying to figure out what is happening inside. He is concentrating and persevering with his interest. He makes lots of noises which can be heard on the tape. I show him how to open and close the door; at first this is difficult, but after my showing him he does it straight away.

When Sam is 18 months old, he uses his remote-control skills when demonstrating how he can write:

Rachel asks him if he wants a pen like Megan. He has one and is given some paper. He enjoys the chalk board and the white board – he likes being able to wipe it off and he will sit for minutes writing and then cleaning it off. Sam's pencil hold is amazing – it is a proper pencil grip.

When Sam is 2 years and 4 months old, he chooses a book, one of his favourite pastimes:

He decides that he wants to go and choose a book. So he goes next door to choose one. He brings in a book and says 'I going to read it' – it is a musical interactive book and he sits and reads with concentration. He sings along with the books – he isn't prompted to do this. He is repeating his actions when he starts to press the stop and then the start button.

When Sam is just 3 years old, the following observation is made:

When I arrive, Sam is on a chair playing with the computer. He has high levels of concentration and he demonstrates good coordination as he uses the mouse to navigate the site that he has chosen. There are levels of skill here that I am surprised to see in a child of Sam's age. Rachel comments that he has developed these skills by playing alongside Liam. She comments that he has got persistence and that he knows what he is trying to do. This becomes clear when he has to explain to us how the program works.

There are now staff in settings who make technology available to very young children, not just the usual cause-and-effect resources that most children would access within the home, but touch-screen computers where they can press objects to create their own picture/ image. In their place, these resources can be very effective and, as the study of Sam demonstrates, his use of remote controls and the computer mouse has also given him the skills to hold a pencil to make marks, using a tripod grip at the age of 18 months old. This is the creativity of the EYFS (DfES, 2007) when it talks about making connections in learning. At the time of writing, Tickell (2011) has just reported on the review of the EYFS with a recommendation that, 'playing and exploring, active learning, and creating and thinking critically are highlighted in the EYFS as three characteristics of effective teaching and learning'. It is hoped that this emphasis remains in any future guidance.

 Questions for reflection

- How could you use your observations to identify children's different schema? Consider how you might adapt your planning to incorporate these.
- How could you adapt your environment to enable 'true' treasure basket and heuristic play to occur as a discrete session?
- How do you create an environment and use resources which encourage young children to use their imagination and to think creatively in their own initiated play?

Further reading

Edwards, C., Gandini, L. and Forman, G. (eds) (1998) *The Hundred Languages of Children,* 2nd edn. London: JAI Press Ltd.

This book reflects upon the approach to creativity in the early years taken in Reggio Emilia, Italy. It looks closely at the history of this approach and describes in detail how practitioners (artelieristi and pedagogista) enable children to engage in long-term investigation through their creativity. This is a core text when thinking of how children learn through creativity.

Goldschmied, E. and Jackson, S. (2004) *People Under Three: Young Children in Day Care,* 2nd edn. London: Routledge.

This book is essential reading for those working with children under 3. It is a core text which gives an overview of the research and rationale behind heuristic play.

Nutbrown, C. (2011) *Threads of Thinking: Young Children Learning and the Role of Early Education*, 4th edn. London: Sage.

This book looks closely at children's schematic play. It is a book with useful case study observations to demonstrate how children learn through schemas. It looks in depth at a complex theory in a readable manner.

References

Athey, C. (2006) *Extending Thought in Young Children: A Parent–Teacher Partnership,* 2nd edn. London: Paul Chapman Publishing.

Department for Education and Skills (DfES) (2007) *Statutory Framework for the Early Years Foundation Stage: Setting the Standards for Learning, Development and Care for Children from Birth to Five.* Nottingham: DfES.

Edwards, C., Gandini, L. and Forman, G. (eds) (1998) *The Hundred Languages of Children,* 2nd edn. London: JAI Press Ltd.

Goldschmied, E. and Jackson, S. (2004) *People Under Three: Young Children in Day Care,* 2nd edn. London: Routledge.

Holland, R. (1997) What's It All About? How Introducing Heuristic Play Has Affected Provision for the Under-threes in One Day Nursery. In L. Abbott and H. Moylett (eds), *Working with Under Threes: Responding to Children's Needs.* Maidenhead: Open University Press.

National Advisory Committee on Creative and Cultural Education (NACCCE) (1999) *All Our Futures: Creativity, Culture and Education.* London: Department for Education and Employment.

Nutbrown, C. (2011) *Threads of Thinking: Young Children Learning and the Role of Early Education,* 4th edn. London: Sage.

Tickell, C. (2011) *The Early Years: Foundations for Life, Health and Learning.* London: DfE. Available at www.education.gov.uk/tickellreview

6

Parents and the Environment

This chapter will:

- discuss the range of choices in childcare
- examine the choices that parents make when choosing day care
- present the experiences of one mother who has accessed a range of day care providers for her children
- reflect on the emotions of parents when leaving their child in the care of others
- discuss parents' feelings and reflections about their choice of nursery once they have left.

Leaving parents and their role in the environment until the end of this book may appear to be an oversight, when parents are the most important influence on children and consequently the vital cog in the wheel, but by examining the other environments first we can then reflect on the parental role.

We continually refer to parents as a child's first educator but how often is this reflected in our practice? It is common to find that we are judgemental about parents, talking about how they never stop to listen and talk; they just drop off their children and leave as if they do not care about their children. This is said without considering the emotional cost to parents when they return to work and have to leave their child in the care of 'strangers'.

> ... it's like if you send pictures home, then its oh another one to stick on the wall and it just seems like you send pictures home and they don't really ... and its going to sound really nasty but its just like they don't care, its just another picture to stick on the wall. (Practitioner)

> Some of them are worried because they are going to get a parking ticket and grab them and go. (Practitioner)

When women had their babies in the past, they used to be cared for by their extended family. I know my mother came to live with me to support me, and in many ways to pass on her experiences. Many of those experiences were invaluable, but looking back, one has to ask the question: are mothers from previous generations necessarily the 'experts'?

I am now a grandmother and my previous experience of having three children would seem to make me one of these 'experts', but things have moved on and I am very mindful of the changes that have occurred in the advice that is given to parents, and mothers in particular.

When visiting a Sure Start Children Centre's Baby Café, it was impressive to observe the way in which young mothers talked, shared experiences and supported one another. They also had the support of an enthusiastic and understanding midwife when they had problems and concerns over breastfeeding. It was whilst sitting listening to these young mothers that the answer to my original question about previous mothers being experts became apparent. Sometimes we are a generation away from the experiences of these women. These networks are perhaps replacing the extended family of the past, and the 'experts' are the other mothers who are having the same experiences in the here and now. Mothers frequently find their own support networks when they begin their maternity leave: through their local Children's Centre, their ante-natal classes and from the National Childbirth Trust. These networks are important to new mothers, as they are able to support each other through a shared experience.

As part of my doctoral research, I interviewed a number of parents prior to my observation of their children. The decision to interview parents was taken because I felt that it was important to understand their reasons for choosing a particular type of childcare and setting. Parental reasons could range from financial necessity to career development, but whatever the reasons for placing a child in an out-of-home care setting, parents need to have trust in the people who are looking after their child. As Goodfellow (2005) recognizes, this choice is a difficult one: 'While guidelines may be provided, the assessment of care is complex and it is often very difficult for parents, as purchasers of care, to assess the quality of care both at the time of searching for a childcare place and during the time when their child is in care.'

Choices of childcare

When I was interviewing other parents, I found that I was influenced by my own personal experiences of when my daughter was 7 months old and I was looking for day care. I initially wanted my daughter to have 1:1 care, but after seeking the advice of others, I was convinced that it was 'safer' for my child to be where there were a number of people to safeguard and protect her. Having reached this decision, choosing the setting was not an issue; a sister-in-law had worked within a setting, the team leader was a personal friend and I also had a 'gut feeling' about the nursery when I walked through the door.

Unlike the mothers of today, when I was choosing day care for my daughter, I was not bombarded by newspaper stories of child abuse, the impact on children's behaviour and generally the whole issue of childcare being put under public scrutiny. Reports of such issues were evident when concerns were raised in *The Guardian* (8 July 2004) about the behaviour of children under the age of 2 in day nurseries: '[there is] mounting evidence that day nurseries for children under the age of two can lead to increased incidence of antisocial behaviour and aggression', and by *The Real Story* programme on BBC1 (12 August 2004) which showed incidences of 'verbal abuse of toddlers, breaches in hygiene and under-staffing … filmed staff shouting at children, and, in one nursery, terms of abuse were used' (BBC News, 2004). Journalistic reports need to be questioned, but must also be taken into account in a society where the media can be a political driver. This opinion was supported by an announcement made in the Ofsted *Early Years Bulletin* (Issue 14, 13 August 2004, www.ofsted.gov.uk) when Maurice Smith stated: 'Although the cases shown in the programme are concerning, we should like to put them in perspective. Such incidents are rare and relate to only a very small number of child carers.'

Is the rarity of such events what we as a society are forgetting when we often damn the whole childcare sector?

These reports are mainly about the stress levels that children had when they attended day care before the age of 2 and little attention was paid to the opinions of mothers. Some of the reports, however, talked to mothers about their experiences with out-of-home care. Many mothers responded positively in the press and this will be later reflected in the opinions of the parents that I interviewed.

> Annette Wiles, who returned to a full time career as a policy manager when her son was 10 months old, feels that working mothers are 'lambasted' for trying to do their best for their children … 'I couldn't be happier with the nursery'. (Henry, 2006, p. 8 *The Sunday Telegraph*, 4 June)

In July 2004, the government announced its Five Year Strategy for Children and Learners with a stated aim as: 'From birth to two, more opportunities for parents to stay at home with their children if they want to ...' (DfES, 2004, p. 6). This prompted me to consider *why* parents choose a private day nursery instead of a childminder, and so when I talked to parents I asked them to offer an explanation around their choices. What was it that parents saw when they visited a nursery? Was it the health and safety? Was it the newness of the setting? Was it something around relationships? Was it something about a setting that appeared to be 'all singing and dancing'?

The role of the childminder as a professional has changed over recent years. The Children Act (1991) has increased the supervision of childminding, which is now regulated by Ofsted and is subject to the same quality inspections as other day care providers. In my involvement with childminders in my professional capacity, I have seen an increase in their attendance at training and have observed the professionalism with which they observe and plan the time that they spend with the babies and young children in their care.

Through my professional life, I have come to see the benefits that caring for a young child in a home environment can have for the child's personal, social and emotional development. Childminding does have its limits because it cannot offer children that wider engagement and interaction with a larger group of children that a pre-school or day nursery can provide. In line with the EPPE (Sylva et al., 2003) research and the *Families, Children and Childcare study* (www.familieschildrenchildcare.org), 'There is considerable evidence in the literature and in this study of relatively poor quality care for infants and toddlers in nurseries' (Leach et al., 2006, p. 32).

A model of childcare that offers parents the opportunity to mix home-based care with group care would be childminding until 2 years old, and then pre-school or day nursery prior to starting formal schooling. This would offer the baby the opportunity to be cared for within a home setting where there could be a more personal relationship with the childminder. This would also be a relationship that had more consistency of care than could be guaranteed within a private day nursery where there has traditionally been a high turnover of staff. Being with a childminder would also give parents the opportunity to have a greater influence over the way in which they wanted their baby to be cared for. It is easier for parents to have this influence, because childminders are with the baby for the whole time (no shift patterns to contend with) and also because the numbers of children being cared for in one environment are smaller. The reason for choosing this mix would be to give a greater opportunity for social interaction and for experiencing being with others in the same environment. I feel that it is important for children at 2 years old to have wider access to a range of resources. If this group provision was accessed on a part-time basis, the child's relationship with the child-minder would be sustained.

The impact of children aged 2 attending day care provision has been recognized by successive UK governments, which have offered targeted children free care of 12 hours a week. The findings have initially shown an increase in children's communication skills.

Reasons for choosing a particular nursery

When I interviewed the parents, I was interested in why they had chosen the particular setting to see if there was a common factor in their responses. The majority of those interviewed stated that they had visited several settings, between two and five, with the exception of one who had only visited one. The reasons for the choices made centered on location, staff, trust and misgivings about accessing childminders.

Location

A common feature for parental choice was the location of the setting. Two out of nine parents had moved nurseries because one had opened up in their locality and two others gave the choice of location for another reason. One parent commented that the particular nursery was near a major road network that she used and therefore this was one of the reasons for making this choice. Two other parents chose it because of its proximity to work. As we previously saw in Chapter 1, the parents had the following reasons:

> It helped me. I often work until 6.00 pm and I looked at the local ones and I would have been struggling if there had been an accident or something. I know they don't dump your child but I didn't want to be late every night. My job gives me free parking opposite the nursery and that is how I saw it. (Mother of Georgina)

> It is very near to work so that if I had to because there was an emergency I can run round in 5 minutes. It is that accessibility as well. (Mother of Melanie)

This close availability was obviously important in making these mothers feel that they could reach their children as quickly as possible in case of emergencies. The location of the setting can cause many problems for parents, especially when they are travelling some distance to work, and it is a factor which providers need to bear in mind when making judgemental comments about the attitudes of parents.

Two sets of parents said that their child had previously been to another setting; the reason for the move had been the establishing of this nursery near to where they lived and also because:

> It [the first setting chosen] seemed OK when I first walked round; it was quiet and calm … when I went to pick him up he was asleep in a rocking chair thing and he never falls asleep in those and they just left him – now if that had been me I would never have left him all hunched over even if it took him time to get back to sleep, I would have made sure he was more comfortable and then he was dead poorly when he came back … and I cried myself to sleep that night. So the next day I went to this nursery. (Mother of Tim)

There was a commonality in the reason why parents had made their initial choice and they responded with comments such as, 'I had just like an instinctive feeling about it' and 'I just got the feeling'. Probing into this matter a little closer, five out of the nine parents interviewed stated that the reason for their choice revolved around the newness of the setting and its resources, the physical building itself and the size of the rooms. This illustrates how important the physical environment discussed earlier is to both children and their parents. What is the reason for different parents' choices? My answer to this will always be: *gut instinct.*

Staff

During the course of the interviews, six out of nine parents who chose one nursery referred to the staff as a factor in their choice of setting when they talked about the ages of the staff. They felt that in many of the nurseries the staff were very young, whereas in this setting there were staff of different ages:

> … I noticed that they all had very young staff and that was one of my main concerns – I can't leave my daughter with 18-year-olds because they've got no experience … [in the chosen setting] there was a mixture. The adult who looked after her had got children and she was a little bit older … she had hands-on experience as opposed to book experience. (Mother of Maisie)

> Another point as well was the staff seemed quite mature people which I liked, it seemed that they were mothers themselves. What put me off other places was that they were quite young, now no discrimination or anything, I know people have got to start somewhere, but to me it was important to me, I felt I could leave her with them and she would be OK. I don't know, it was just the experience came across very well that they had and that was the key thing. (Mother of Harriet)

This comment about the older member of staff was very revealing, especially as she was unqualified but with a wealth of experience.

Another factor in one nursery was that one of the nursery assistants was male. Two of the parents commented on this during the interviews. One parent saw it immediately as a positive:

> P wasn't there when we first went … I think it's quite good they are not just getting the female side of things. You've got a mixture, particularly if you've got boys. I think it is brilliant. I think it is fantastic; I really, really do, especially the little boys … I think it's a big thing for the lads. I think there should be more of them to be honest. He's fantastic, absolutely fantastic. Gets on the floor, he's like a dad really on the floor, he has them all climbing on his back. He was playing football today with them, you know things like that. It's nice. (Mother of Harriet)

Desire to further their children's social development

Another interesting response to come out of the parent interviews was that many of the parents expressed their unwillingness to put their children in full time day care: 'No one was good enough to look after my daughter'; 'I think even if it's the best nursery in the world you don't want to send them, you want to stay at home with her …', but several of them also balanced this with the desire for their children to be engaged with other children for social interaction. Two parents commented on their sister's children not having attended anywhere and who now find it difficult to mix. One parent expressed the social interaction as the main reason for her son attending nursery, because he was showing signs of not accepting the presence of other children or adults. For this mother, I would say that the nursery fulfilled this need, as her son approached and initiated talk with adults and other children using his excellent vocabulary skills.

The comments from parents about the importance of social interaction and development were interesting in that parents felt that the development of children's social skills within the nursery was important: '... to mix with other kids, to develop her communication skills and just to muck in', but when questioned about the children's learning, they placed care and safety as their highest criteria: '... because he's so young I just want to be able to go to work just knowing that he's safe and being looked after'; 'I think it is a combination but at this age it is the care. I think care is the main one'.

One of the parents made an interesting statement about one of the criteria she used when looking for a day care setting for her daughter:

I actually wanted her to mix with children of mixed race and to be in an area that has got mixed cultures, and I thought a nursery would be better for that ... I was asking them about how they treated Christmas and Eid and all of the various religious festivals. Cultural diversity is a key thing that I would like her to be exposed to. (Mother of Melanie)

This was interesting in that as part of her research into nurseries, she read Ofsted reports to see if there was any mention of cultural diversity within them. This parent was the only one of those interviewed who stated that they had referred to the Ofsted website (www.ofsted. gov.uk) to help them in their search for a nursery.

Choice of day nursery over childminder

When talking to mothers about their choice of childcare, many of them refer to the question of trust. Interestingly, this comment is always made when making reference to putting babies and young children into the care of childminders. As a young mother I was ignorant of how to access day care, and I also fell into the trap of associating single adult care as fraught with lack of safety and protection.

The following comments from parents refer to this fear about accessing care where there is only one adult present:

With a day nursery you have got more security. Security because if you don't know the childminder personally and it's on a one to one basis you don't really know what they are doing. They could be doing anything to your child. (Mother of Tim)

We didn't have a childminder because of the safety factor. (Mother of Ben)

The reason I did not put him with a childminder or a nanny was that I was a bit scared of leaving him with just one person that I didn't know. You would get to know them over time but it would take longer than a few months. Nurseries are more controlled, there are more people. They are audited and then from time to time there are inspections. (Mother of Martin)

Another parent, although concerned about the safety factors involved when using a childminder, did recognize that there could be advantages in her child forming a more personal relationship with one individual.

I was going to go to a childminder because I thought Dan would have that personal 1:1 contact but after speaking to friends – I did actually go to visit a childminder, she was lovely – she was quite young although she was qualified, she had her own child and one other child and I just got the feeling that she was putting a lot of her energies into her own child and I just thought that it is somebody's house and I am sure everything would be fine but you don't know what she does when I am not there. There are no other adults around to keep an eye on the place and I just felt she was putting quite a lot of her attention onto her own child and Dan might be second – second best almost. My first consideration was actually a childminder but having visited her and gone through that thought process, I decided that a nursery would be better because he would have the interaction of other children and there would be other staff there. (Mother of Dan)

Another mother stated that, from the start, she was sceptical of childminders. Her response shows her lack of knowledge about the registration and inspection of childminders, which raises concerns about the way in which this information is disseminated to parents.

I am a bit sceptical about childminders and when I looked into it about a year ago there didn't seem to be any safeguards, no checks. As I understand it people can just go on a register and there is no checking of those people and so I didn't have any confidence about picking someone off a register. You can go and meet them but then Melanie would be with two or three other children and they would be in her house. I just didn't like the idea of a childminder. Somebody who has got no strictures, there's no control over them. A couple of people that I know have had bad experiences and so I did not want to go down that road. (Mother of Melanie)

When looking at these comments from parents about childminders, it is interesting to reflect on their opinions. What is it about accessing a childminder that is so intimidating when they are subject to the same rigours of inspection as day nurseries? Childminders today are also expected to have higher levels of qualifications, but do parents still see this as someone just taking in other people's children whilst they stay at home to look after their own children? Not a proper job? Is this the reason for the low regard from these parents when referring to childminders? The work of the National Childminding Association (NCMA) has done much to raise the status of childminders, but I feel that although in the recent past policy makers and governments have seen the importance of childminding, it is important to continue to champion their role in the day care sector.

Other parents' responses show that they were ambivalent about using a childminder but that, upon reflection, they feel that they have made the right choice in choosing a day nursery.

> I mean to start with I couldn't decide, I was actually going to put him with a childminder, I just didn't know what to do for the best. I'm so glad we decided as we did. (Mother of James)

> I was more comfortable with day care than a childminder. (Mother of Tim)

These comments show that these particular parents had made a positive decision to use a day nursery and that the reason for that decision made them feel positive about their experiences within the nursery.

It is interesting that many of the media headlines now refer to the fact that there are safety concerns within nursery provision where there are a number of adults present. Is this just because, as a society, we hear of such concerns because news is far more readily available? Are things any less safe for our children than they were in the past or are we just more vigilant?

One mother's experiences in accessing a range of childcare

Rachel, Sam's mother, gave an interesting perspective on accessing the different types of day care provision, as with her previous two children she had accessed a childminder, a day nursery and a pre-school, when she returned to work. Her comments about how this felt were interesting in that she commented on the difficulties involved in selecting someone to care for your child in their home.

> It just seemed to me such a personal thing and that when I actually came to think about childminders I was overwhelmed by the fact that you almost had to interview the childminder and I'm not very comfortable with that sort of thing because I find it very hard to sort of well to be critical of people really, when I appreciate there are different ways of doing things and I sort of vaguely knew what I was looking for but at that time wouldn't have known how to probe that through questions, so I wasn't really comfortable with going through the whole interview process of childminders so I think I assumed that I would go to private day nursery …

Following on from this, Rachel had her decision questioned when a colleague recommended a childminder. This information meant that Rachel could go into the childminder's home without these initial worries:

> … one of my colleagues said that their child was leaving the childminder and a very local childminder close to where we used to live. I decided that I felt comfortable enough to go and talk to her about it and just basically when I went in just felt like that she was able to tell me much more than I was needing to ask her, she gave me a lot of information to start with.

Having decided to go though with this 'interview' process, Rachel was able to come to a decision without pressure:

> She showed me things; she showed me pictures of the children, the whole, basically had a guided tour of the house, where everything was. It just made me feel, she put me at ease really and made me actually, I suppose she was selling to me but basically in a way that made me feel I was under no pressure whatsoever and I didn't feel like, I almost felt like I had to grab her because I felt like she was not desperately wanting to have me because there would be other people that she could find so she wasn't desperate for children and that made me feel a bit better, the fact that she wasn't pushing me to make any decision at all, she left it open she gave me sort of a 2/3 week window to make a decision to go back and have another look and I actually went back when she had the children with her and took Liam and he just looked so settled with the whole thing.

When I asked Rachel if this had been a joint decision between herself and her husband, she commented that if they had been going to look at day nurseries, Neil would have been involved, but he felt that with a childminder it was much more of a personal issue and that it was Rachel who needed to build up these relationships, especially as his job meant that he worked shift patterns. Rachel herself later commented on this personal aspect when I asked her about the advantages or disadvantages of using a childminder:

> I think the pros are that, very much that personal relationship and the fact that you do basically get the ins and outs of everything that has gone on in the day. You can see the sort of relationship building with the childminder and especially when they are that much younger that was really important, it was obviously that thing of going back to work in the first place and knowing that Liam was happy with somebody and they would be the person that got to know him and his bits and what he liked and everything and the way he liked to do things.

The only disadvantage that Rachel felt with using a childminder was the breaking of this relationship. For Rachel, this problem did not arise because when her son was 2, a time when she felt that he needed more than the childminder could offer, they moved areas and she was on maternity leave expecting her daughter. This meant that when they moved, her son was able to access a day nursery and when she returned to work when her daughter was 9 months old, she also began to attend.

This meant that Rachel had used both a day nursery and a childminder and I was interested in her reasons for choosing a day nursery and how she felt this experience compared with the childminder. Her responses show that choice is sometimes a luxury; she was moving areas in November and was looking for places for both children and frequently her choice was restricted by the availability of places. I asked her about the criteria that she employed when visiting places and also for her reflections on the different nurseries. Her first response referred to the appearance of the setting:

> One of the ones I went to was a very new nursery that was set up and that I didn't take to really. The staff were very, very young obviously, all new – beautiful place, beautiful set-up, very well resourced and the person who showed me round, she was probably the manager, was very good at sort of selling but I wasn't convinced that what I was seeing matched up with what I was being told and although to be fair it was early stages, they were setting up.

As Rachel developed her response, she made reference to the staff and their interactions with the children, which is reminiscent of the responses from the other parents interviewed:

There were just things like they didn't stop talking when I went in the room, they were all chatting amongst themselves and the children were playing. I thought well if they are not going to do that when I go in and you know have any expectations that that was what you might do when there was a parent coming round or that they weren't necessarily going to be doing that when I wasn't there and when the children were there.

When she visited the next nursery, the official regime had an impact on her decision:

So I wasn't really happy with that and the other one I went to see I just felt that I was being given too many rules really of how I would be expected to behave. The things like the pick-up times mattered, the payment – all those things were what came across to me rather than actually getting me to feel for the nursery and then make those decisions afterwards. So I just felt that the priorities were slightly different.

In making her final decision, Rachel weighed up all of these disadvantages and ultimately felt that she did not have much of a choice; her dislike of factors in other settings made her select the 'best of the bunch':

So the one we went for in the end just seemed to balance those things really; there were those things to discuss but I was given as long as I wanted really to look round, ask questions and just felt that the children looked as if they were engaged all the time, they were focused and it was a really happy atmosphere. So I didn't really have a huge range of choice but that one stood out for me.

In her reflections on the effectiveness for her children, Rachel stated:

I think it was a great setting. There are always things that perhaps you would do differently or that you would ask to have different but given that they were catering for the needs of so many different children, so many different families, there wasn't a huge turnover of staff, there was consistency, Liam loved it and he is a really fussy child in terms of, he would let me know if there was – he isn't backwards in coming forwards if he doesn't like something. The fact that he enjoyed it, you know they were both upset when they left. I feel that it was a very positive experience for them and it was definitely the right choice to make at the time.

Having had the experiences of a childminder and a day nursery for her first two children, Rachel decided not to return to work when Sam was born. Having made this decision, her daughter, Megan, left the day nursery to start at a local playgroup, whilst Liam had started to attend the local maintained nursery school. Rachel made the following comments about Megan's time in the playgroup:

> She's just started, she does a couple of afternoons. I love that. I think that's my favourite set-up really. I think it's because she has a bit of both really, I have the time at home with her but the playgroup has got a very good reputation that she goes to and it's fantastic, it's only a church hall, but it's all set up and with access to all the things that you have in nursery apart from outdoor play, that's the only thing they can't do but she's only there for two and a half hours and she absolutely loves it. She's only been there a few weeks and I thought she might have difficulties because she's been at home with me for five months and I thought she might struggle with me and going somewhere new but they do have this parent and toddler group there that she's been going to with me so she's used to being in the place and she's seen the staff and now she's sort of progressed up to being there on her own.

When reflecting on all of these childcare experiences, I asked Rachel what she felt to have been the best combination and why:

> Yes [the part-time playgroup sessions with the rest of time spent within the home] I think so; I think it allows for the best of both worlds really. I say that Liam really needed more than the childminder in the home but private day nursery which was basically 8.00 to 5.30 I felt was too long and so to have a bit of both and to have access to group situations and all the resources and all the things that are there in that setting for short periods of time and at her age is ideal ... In terms of functioning with their peers and all the things about independence and her actually experiencing that life is different from being just with me and that she has to negotiate things and that she has to put up with things that she wouldn't choose to do but she actually, I think those have been the real benefits of it that they've actually grown up in a different way than they would have with me and that that hasn't undermined anything that I've done.

Rachel goes on further to relate the benefits of this mixed system to the benefits that it has given her children when they have started to attend full-time school in the maintained sector, and also of the exposure to the approaches of different people, which she feels gives her children a more flexible approach to the adults that they come into contact with:

> It's just been a different way and I think in terms of them being ready to go to school that flexibility of being able to adapt to different situations, different people's expectations and ways of managing them and the opportunities they get – I mean even the way people discuss things or approach things completely different from how I would and I just think the benefits of that must be huge.

These comments did not mean that Rachel had negative feelings about her use of the childminder; on the contrary, she felt that she could not replicate the experiences that she had had with Liam's childminder:

> ... but only a certain type of childminder, I wouldn't have just gone to the childminder for the sake of it. If I hadn't have been happy with it I think I would have preferred day nurseries better than a childminder I wasn't 100% happy with so to have the luxury of a fantastic childminder was great.

Rachel's experiences give an insight into the dilemmas of choosing childcare and how some of these choices can impact in an emotional way. When I talked to other mothers, I was struck by the rawness of their emotions, even though the children of some of them had begun attending the nurseries some time before I talked to them.

The emotions of parents

When I specifically asked the parents about how they felt when their baby first started to attend the nursery, the majority of them talked about their distress at leaving their child in the care of others. This feeling of distress was expressed in many ways. One mother talked about her feelings of guilt:

> I think the fact that he is not with mum all that time, I sometimes feel a bit guilty about the fact that I do have to leave him there as much as it does have its benefits, they are your babies and you want them to be with you all the time, but then I don't think I could necessarily be a full-time mum. I think it is just getting that balance right really. (Mother of Dan)

Others expressed their feelings of not liking the situation and of having to have made this choice in the first place:

> I think even if it's the best nursery in the world you don't want to send them, you want to stay at home with her. (Mother of Amy)

> I didn't like any of them to be honest with you. I was having traumas with all of them. To be honest I didn't want to leave her anywhere but it was the best of them all. (Mother of Maisie)

> If I didn't have to work full time I wouldn't put her in a nursery. I am somebody who would never have thought would say that. I would chat with friends before and say I will be dying to get back to work but I actually enjoy seeing her develop and playing with her. I don't tidy up all the time, I leave things around so she can play. I am able to work but if I had a choice I wouldn't. I don't know how long it would last for, I would probably get bored after a bit. (Mother of Melanie)

For some mothers, their feelings about leaving their children were more demonstrative and their comments show the emotional pull on them:

> I felt terrible about leaving her at nursery. I burst into tears when I got into the car on the way back. You just think I am not that kind of person, how could I be so pathetic but at the same time it was good to know that I could ring the nursery. (Mother of Melanie)

> I was worried sick like should I call, I can't remember if I did actually call, rang them about an hour after she was in just in case. (Mother of Harriet)

> The first couple of months he used to cry and I found that heart wrenching. (Mother of James)

These comments illustrate how hard it is for parents to leave their children in the care of others. Interestingly, although some fathers were present at the interviews, all of the above comments were made by mothers. It seems that no matter what the quality of the setting and no matter how certain mothers are in their choice of setting, they all have a guilty feeling about having to put their child into care. These feelings of guilt are not helped by writers such as Biddulph (2006, p. 13), who states in answer to the question to parents about whether to use a day nursery:

- Earning and spending have become more important in our world than caring and communicating with those around us. Today's world runs on greed and speed.
- Childhood has changed, with much less time available and less sense of family and community. The heavy use of day nurseries for very young children is just one symptom of this.
- Your big decisions in life are between money and love. If you put love first, it changes everything.

These comments make no reference to the distress that parents, mothers in particular, struggle with when making these decisions. On the other hand, Waldfogel (2006) recognizes that there is no universal answer to the question, as for some children having access to good quality and consistent day care may be preferable to staying at home with their mothers. Mothers may be the primary caregiver, but sometimes even the best of mothers need some respite which may be of benefit to both mother and child. Many writers today criticize mothers for putting their children into day care without looking closely at some of the benefits for mother and child.

The findings from The Equality and Human Rights Commission research report, *Childcare: A Review of What Parents Want* (Campbell-Barr and Garnham, 2010), recognizes that when parents, and mothers in particular, are making choices about childcare, they are aware of what they believe goes towards making a good mother. This conflict can have a strain on working mothers as they are faced with the dilemma of being both a good mother and a good worker (Vincent et al., 2008). This is reminiscent of the notion of the 'good-enough mother' (Winnicott, 2005) where the mother adapts to her baby's needs, both physically and emotionally, and who over time supports her child to become aware that he is an individual and separate from his mother.

Guendouzi (2006) identifies that the role of working mothers has changed whilst society's image of this mothering role has not and that this influences the 'guilty' feeling that many women experience when placing their child in an out-of-home setting. It is this conflict that Guendouzi recognizes as an area for further research: 'Research on working mothers should lead to a better understanding of why the "guilt thing" still has such a strong influence. Discourses reflecting and recycling a model of intensive mothering need to give way to discourses that better reflect the reality of modern women's lives.' Mothers of babies and young children frequently spend their precious maternity leave worrying about their return to work; surely this emotional trauma for mothers needs to be recognized in all the work that we do with supporting families back to work.

Parents' reflections

When looking at parents' reasons for accessing childcare, it is also interesting to look at what their feelings were when their children left the provision. I therefore composed an exit questionnaire to ascertain these emotions, asking parents to reflect on their experiences.

I would like you to reflect on the time that your child spent in day care.

Name of child:

Nursery attended:

Reason for child leaving nursery (if they have left):

If your child transferred where did he/she go to:

Please rate your experiences at the nursery (where 1 is GOOD and 5 is POOR):

1   2   3   4   5

If you would like to, please make comments about why you have rated the nursery in this way:

Briefly describe the strengths (if any) of the nursery:

(Continued)

(Continued)

Briefly describe the weaknesses (if any) of the nursery:

If you had another child, would you like them to attend the same nursery:

YES   NO

If NO, please state why not:

Did you have any regrets about sending your child to a day nursery?

If you were asked for any suggestions that you could make in order to improve the nursery and its service to you and your family, what would they be?

Please feel free to make any additional comments in the space below:

Thank you for taking the time to complete this form.

Figure 6.1　Exit questionnaire

These exit interviews were very interesting. Among the responses of those parents that were contactable after they had left the nursery, many of them were quite critical in their reflections on the setting and what it had offered them and their children:

> When Mark finished we got an incomplete folder of stuff that the staff could not be bothered to complete or communicate to us. (Father of Mark)

The parents of Amy were very critical when asked to express their opinions of the nursery and the service that they had received once their daughter had left the baby rooms:

> ... care was very poor and communication between staff and parents was non-existent. Teenagers looked after the children, whilst more experienced and mature staff seemed to leave or be promoted to managers and do clerical duties.

These reflections were evident in all of the returns from one of the case study nurseries, where there were comments about the age of the staff. This is ironic as many of these parents had chosen this particular nursery because of the range of ages of the staff. These parents commented on the high turnover of the staff and the lack of communication. All respondents to the questionnaire commented on the strength of the care and communication in the baby rooms: 'The care was very good downstairs but was poor upstairs.' Could this be that when parents are first choosing a nursery, they are focusing on the care and the relationships with staff in the baby room, and pay very little or no attention to the structure of the whole nursery? Or could this be where nurseries feel more comfortable in what they are offering to parents of babies; knowing that parents of babies need to have communication about their baby's day in care, especially around the routines of feeding and nappy changing, whereas when the children are older, the staff lack the confidence to talk to parents about how their children are learning and developing? One parent made a comment which I felt to be revealing in regard to the confidence of the staff:

> I think all nurseries should have a qualified teacher who is there every morning to greet the children ... (Parents of Amy)

This comment is particularly interesting in that it is reflective of the research findings from the EPPE project and is one of the policies that the coalition government (2010) is retaining from the Labour government's childcare agenda. In both the Frank Field (2010) and Graham Allen (2011) reports, they recognize the need to strengthen the workforce with graduates.

The comments in the exit questionnaire from the parents who attended the nursery based in one room are more positive:

> Always been happy with the nursery. Georgina has always enjoyed herself and I have been happy with care. Very professional. Varied activity programme. I am certain that nursery had a positive effect on Georgina and contributed to her outgoing and sociable personality. (Mother of Georgina)

> The care Martin received in the two years was excellent. It has helped Martin to develop his personality and give him confidence to become a very sociable, independent and happy child. Very open, approachable staff. Big family style approach. Close and personal care for the children. Very flexible. Safe. (Mother of Martin)

There is a marked difference in these reflective accounts of experience, especially when compared to the parents' views when they first chose a setting for their children.

What does the second nursery do that the first does not? During the period of conducting the case studies, there was very little movement of staff within this nursery. The nursery offered a more family style of care, so that all of the children were in the same room. Is this the reason why the parents are more positive about the service they have been offered? Is it also that the parents are more familiar with the staff? Is the family-style approach more positive for parents and their relationships with the staff because they see the entire environment on a daily basis? When these parents chose this nursery, they were able to see the whole nursery in operation rather than just the baby room; they could see what was to follow from their first visit to the nursery, whereas in the other nursery the parents are really only familiar with the baby room because this was where they spent their time when their baby was first settling in.

⌇⌇ Questions for reflection

- Read the following extract from Nutbrown and Page (2008, pp. 181–7) and consider your attitude to love when working with babies and young children. Does this attitude have any impact on your relationships with parents?

- What is the philosophy of your setting when it comes to parental involvement in creating and influencing the environments?
- Discuss ways in which your setting involves parents in their children's learning. What do you do well, and what else could you be doing? Consider the approaches that you use and question whether these are really about a partnership, or about a way of disseminating information to parents?

Further reading

Abbott, L. and Langston, A. (eds) (2006) *Parents Matter: Supporting the Birth to Three Matters: Framework*. Maidenhead: Open University Press.
This book explores the relationships that should develop between nurseries and parents. It looks at the role of the parents and the extended family in a young child's life.

Nutbrown, C. and Page, J. (2008) *Working with Babies and Children: From Birth to Three*. London: Sage.
This book is essential reading for those working with children under 3. It includes insightful reflections on the relationships between care providers and parents.

Waldfogel, J. (2006) *What Children Need*. London: Harvard University Press.
This book looks at childcare arrangements in the USA and at how the choices and emotional needs of parents should be met.

References

Allen, G. (2011) *Early Intervention: The Next Steps. An Independent Report to Her Majesty's Government*. London: The Stationery Office.

Biddulph, S. (2006) *Raising Babies: Should Under 3s go to Nursery?* London: HarperThorsons.

Bunting, M. (2004) *Fear on Nursery Care Forces Rethink*. Available at www.guardian.co.uk/uk/2004/jul/08/research.children

Cambell-Barr, V. and Garnham, A. (2010) *Childcare: A Review of What Parents Want*. Manchester: Equality and Human Rights Commission.

Department for Education and Skills (DfES) (2004) *Five Year Strategy for Children and Learners*. London: HMSO.

Field, F. (2010) *The Foundation Years: Preventing Poor Children Becoming Poor Adults*. London: Cabinet Office.

Goodfellow, J. (2005) Market Childcare: Preliminary Considerations of a 'Property View' of the Child. *Contemporary Issues in Early Childhood*, 6(1): 54–65.

Guendouzi, J. (2006) 'The Guilt Thing': Balancing Domestic and Professional Roles. *Journal of Marriage and Family*, 68: 901–9.

Henry, J. (2006) 'A Third More Babies Left in Full-time Care', *The Sunday Telegraph*, 4 June. Available at: www.telegraph.co.uk/news/uknews/1520248/A-third-more-babies-left-in-full-time-care.html

Leach, P., Barnes, J., Malmberg, L., Sylva, K., Stein, A. and the FCCC team (2006) *The Quality of Different Types of Child Care at 10 and 18 Months: A Comparison Between Types and Factors Related to Quality*. Available at www.familieschildrenchildcare org/fccc_frames_home.html

Nutbrown, C. and Page, J. (2008) *Working with Babies and Children: From Birth to Three*. London: Sage.

Sylva, K., Meluish, E., Sammons, P., Siraj-Blatchford, I., Taggart, B. and Elliot, K. (2003) *The Effective Provision of Pre-School Education (EPPE) Project: Findings from the Pre-School Period* (Research Brief No: RBX15-03). London: DfES Publications.

Vincent, C., Ball, S. and Braun, A. (2008) *Local Childcare Cultures: Working Class Families and Pre-school Childcare*. London: Institute of Education/ESRC.

Waldfogel, J. (2006) *What Children Need*. London: Harvard University Press.

Winnicott, D.W. (2005) *Playing and Reality*. London: Routledge.

Useful websites

www.familieschildrenchildcare.org
www.ncma.org.uk
www.ofsted.gov.uk

7 Observing and Questioning

This chapter will:

- look at the value of observing practice
- offer a framework to question all aspects of the environment, including the involvement of the adult
- discuss learning stories and offer a framework for tracking babies and young children's development
- reflect on the questions raised throughout the book.

It is universally recognized that the best way in which to identify next steps for children's learning is to carry out meaningful observations. What many of us do not do, however, is apply the same principle to our own practice. Many of the accredited Quality Assurance schemes build peer observations into the process and it is increasingly being recognized that this is the way forward for encouraging practitioners to become reflective.

Practitioners who worked on the Every Child a Talker national initiative (ECaT, 2009) worked with consultants to improve their interactions with children. Many used video cameras to capture their interactions, and then played them back to focus on how they were giving children the opportunity to engage. When these observations were first carried out, many practitioners were shocked by the way in which they dominated the talking space and at how directional they were within their interactions and involvement. If we, as practitioners, use methods of observation to not only assess children's learning but also to reflect upon our own practice, we will be ensuring better quality experiences for the children in our care.

The use of modern technology to conduct these observations is one way but many people are reluctant to be filmed, and when they are, they are frequently very self-conscious and so do not interact with the children in a natural manner. In order for the process to become part of everyday practice, the camera will have to be used on many occasions until it becomes part of the daily routine. When practitioners are filmed, it is important that an agreement about confidentiality and its use is established. The ideal is for the practitioner being filmed to watch it back with a room leader or manager and then to have an open and non-judgemental discussion about what is being observed. The idea of the observation is not to find fault but to establish areas for development.

When I conducted my research, I did not use filming of the children as a method, as this was fraught with data protection and ethical issues around the children whom I did not have permission to observe. It was therefore decided to take snapshot photographs of the children for whom parental consent had been obtained, to support the long observations that were carried out. An original thought was to use an existing analytical framework to assist with the analysis of the observations, such as the Thomas Coram Research Unit Group (TCRU) Care Observation checklist (Thomas Coram Research Unit, 2002, Research on Ratios, Group Size and Staff Qualifications and Training in Early Years and Childcare Settings, DfES, 2002), which although useful when conducting large-scale research projects, did not suit my purpose.

Using the Early Childhood Environment Rating Scale (ECERS-E) (Sylva et al., 2006) and Infant/Toddler Environmental Rating Scale (ITERS-R) (Harms et al., 2003) was also considered as a framework. These rating scales are invaluable when looking at the whole environment rather than at individual children. These environmental audits assist with evaluating the environment in which the children are involved. I found that these scales did not enable me to look at individual children and how the environment impacted on them. I have, however, used these scales within my authority to help identify areas for development and have found them very useful in forming an action plan for the setting to move forwards. As these audits are rigid and measurable, they give an objective view of the setting which is important when identifying areas for development at feedback. The ECERS audits have a reputation for providing a quality evaluation and they have been used both nationally and internationally to evaluate research programmes (Sylva et al., 2004; Mathers and Sylva, 2007; Mathers et al., 2007).

Framework

After due consideration of all the possible frameworks that could be used, it was concluded that already recognized frameworks did not suit the needs of this particular research and so I decided to look at how the *Birth to Three Matters* framework (DfES, 2002) could be used to analyse the observations. I developed a system using *Birth to Three Matters* (DfES, 2002) to evaluate the observations against the national document to see whether it met the needs of practitioners. The system was developed by selecting the major themes in *Birth to Three Matters* (DfES, 2002) to ask questions. The decision was taken to use the major themes of *Birth to Three Matters* (DfES, 2002) because at the time this was the core national document which all settings were using. It was also a document which I had been using with practitioners with some mixed success. I, therefore, decided to use the framework in order to challenge my own misgivings to see if it could answer my research questions with particular reference to the role of adults' contribution to the experiences of children, parents and practitioners.

The observations that had been gathered over time were taken and placed into the framework of questions shown in Figure 7.1. Over the years, this framework has been refined to use in different aspects of my professional role but it has always proved the most useful tool for observing babies and children under 3 years of age. The questions can be helpful in focusing your observations and enabling you to write notes alongside. When writing up the observation from the nursery or childminder's home, the notes are fed into the framework, leaving in the questions so that the practitioner can easily see what was being looked for. It is important that the setting and the practitioners appreciate that you have recognized that this is a snapshot observation, hence writing *not evidenced* in answer to those questions where there has been no observation of practice or interaction is important. By leaving the question in, it means that the manager or childminder can then see what was being looked for and ask themselves, *Does this actually happen?* This is important because, frequently, we assume that something is happening.

As can be seen from the framework, I have relied heavily on looking at the core areas for babies and toddlers: Personal, Social and Emotional Development, including the key focus of Relationships, Communication and Language, and Active Learning, which looks at cognitive development. This is in line with the recommendations of Tickell (2011) when she states '... that personal, social and emotional development, communication and language and physical development are identified as prime areas of learning in the EYFS'. One area of development that is a focus for babies and young children is physical, but as these observations are a snapshot it is difficult to come to any conclusions about the physical development of individuals.

The following case study illustrates how I fed in the observations of Tim to look at his physical development over time, in this case

Personal, Social and Emotional Development

Are babies/children free to express feelings of joy/grief/frustration/fear?
Are experiences of primary caregivers respected?
Is the physical environment clean/safe/uncluttered?
Are resources age-appropriate?
Are babies/children able to explore through movement?
Are babies/children encouraged to be independent?
Do babies/children experience their environment from different levels/perspectives?
Do babies/children explore through their senses?
Are babies/children offered a balanced diet?
Is the environment conducive for babies/children to rest and sleep?
Do adults respond with affection when babies/children are distressed?

Communication and Language

Do babies/children make eye contact/touch/vocalize with other babies/children and adults?
Do adults have good relationships with parents/carers? How is this evidenced?
Does the environment encourage a variety of 'conversations' to take place?
Do adults model language by echoing?
Do adults respond to babies/children's own language by interpreting it?
Do adults create situations for babies/children to communicate?
Do adults role-model language for babies/children whilst playing etc.?
Do adults use language/songs/stories to communicate with babies/children?
Do adults 'attempt' to understand babies/children's language?
Do adults respond to babies/children's interests?
Do adults give babies/children choices?

Active Learning

Do babies/children explore through: touch/sight/sound/taste/smell/movement?
Do adults repeat activities for babies/children?
Are babies/children active or passive learners?
Are babies/children encouraged to be curious?
Do adults respond to the cues of the play of babies/children?
Are babies/children able to express themselves through the 'hundred languages of children'?
Are babies/children given opportunities to imitate?
Do adults give babies/children time to persevere?
Do adults encourage babies/children to mark make in a variety of ways?
Do adults provide opportunities for children to match, sort, classify and categorize?
Do babies/children have opportunities to engage with role play?

(Continued)

Relationships

Have babies/children formed attachments with adults?
Are feeding/sleep routines individual to babies?
Do babies/children have 1:1 contact time?
How are babies/children encouraged to explore and investigate?
How do adults respond to babies/children's actions, expressions and gestures?
How does the setting give 'personal space' to babies/children?

Principles of Practice

Parents and families are central to the wellbeing of the child.
Relationships with other people (both adults and children) are of crucial importance in a child's life.
A relationship with a key person at home and in the setting is essential to young children's wellbeing.
Babies and young children are social beings and they are competent learners from birth.
Learning is a shared process and children learn most effectively when, with the support of a knowledgeable and trusted adult, they are actively involved and interested.
Caring adults count more than resources and equipment.
Schedules and routines must flow with the child's needs.
Children learn when they are given appropriate responsibility, allowed to make errors, decisions and choices, and respected as autonomous and competent learners.
Children learn by doing rather than by being told.
Young children are vulnerable. They learn to be independent by having someone they can depend upon.

Figure 7.1 A framework for analysing observations and practice

17 months. Due to the extended period of this case study, I would suggest that it is appropriate to look at a child's individual physical development. The case study clearly shows the progress that Tim is making in his development.

Case study 25: Observations carried out on Tim between the ages of 16 months and 2 years 9 months

Are babies/children able to explore through movement?

- Tim becomes very interested in picking the pasta out of the bowl. His pincer movement is very good and he is precise in his movements.

(Continued)

(Continued)

- He puts one of the discs on his head and tries to balance it.
- He is a physically active child – more interested in movement and investigation than engaging in talk – he looks closely at things and explores his environment.
- When he first gets outside, Tim does a run around the area.
- Tim then picks up a ball which he kicks around – he shows good coordination as he kicks the ball.
- Tim then turns his attention to getting in and out of the car.
- After this, Tim goes over to the ball pool and jumps in; he then goes through a series of getting in and out of the pool – Tim is really enjoying this play; he is excited when he falls onto the balls. Prior to jumping in, he swings his arms back and forth before leaping/diving into the pool. Now when he is preparing to dive in, you can see that he is mouthing '1, 2, 3 jump' to himself.
- In the ball pool play, Tim really challenges himself physically – he is confident in what he can do and is well coordinated.
- He starts to put glue on his paper and then goes to gather up the spilt glitter. He has good pincer movement and good hand-to-eye coordination as he is doing this.
- Tim is very animated outside and is playing and interacting with all of the other children. He becomes involved in a game with Amy.
- During this game, Tim shows that he has good coordination – he is also good at balancing.
- A group of children, including Tim, go over to where the mattresses are stacked and start climbing and jumping on and off them. This is a similar gross motor play to that Tim was engaged with on the last observation.

Another reason for having a focus on these areas of development is that I personally have always struggled with some of the descriptors of the EYFS (DfES, 2007) when applying them to babies and young children under 3 years of age. For instance, it is hard to look for evidence of babies' development in Writing, Handwriting, Reading, Problem Solving, Reasoning and Numeracy. These are all terms which are not readily associated with babies and young children and are areas which many practitioners struggle with. A good example of this is when practitioners are looking at cultures, for instance Chinese New Year, and they have this planned into the babies' learning objectives. Practitioners need to challenge this practice in their settings and ask themselves how a baby of 9 months old can have any understanding of such an event? The following case study illustrates what we should be looking for when working with the youngest children. This study tracks Tim's development in establishing relationships.

Case study 26: Observations carried out on Tim between the ages of 17 months and 2 years 9 months

Do babies/children make eye contact/touch/vocalize with other babies/children and adults?

- Some of the other children have gone to play on the see-saws and Tim stands and watches them closely.
- He stands up and looks at me intently – he maintains his gaze as he walks back towards the adult sitting at the painting.
- He makes good eye contact with the adult.
- When he gets out of the car, Tim walks over to the climbing frame and stands facing another child on the other side. He bangs the tarpaulin sheet and stretches it – he bangs the tarpaulin and laughs. Tim runs about with another child making da, da, da noises – then there are three of them doing this. There is lots of laughter during this period.
- Tim then makes eye contact with me and stares for a few seconds. When he walks into the room, he goes to stand near another child – it looks as though the two of them are having a conversation. They both look over to me and make sounds – these sounds get louder and louder, they are playing a game with one another and with me. Tim is very happy; he is smiling, enjoying this game and enjoying vocalizing with the other boy. The two of them stand for a while and shout at me.
- When it is snack time, Tim is very sociable, he plays with his neighbour and shares his snack with her.
- He joins in when another child starts shouting.
- He goes to join some other children at a table and then leaves.
- Amy and Tim start to engage with one another. As the observation will show, the two of them are very close – they do a lot together and they share jokes with one another. They both go into the ball pool and then they both climb out. Amy follows Tim until she crashes into someone else. Amy and Tim are now playing together and they return to the ball pool.

(Continued)

(Continued)

- The two of them continue to follow one another around as they play – they have moved on from parallel play to cooperative play – this is a real friendship.
- This observation has seen a change in Tim – he is boisterous, interested, more social and he has moved on from parallel play to a definite social play – the social play and friendship between Tim and Amy is almost visible.
- Tim goes to find Amy and they cuddle and tickle one another.
- Amy and Tim now play hiding with the cloths and the muslin and they play peekaboo with the adult.
- Tim is enjoying the social interactions and the physicality of the game – this is a game for boys; there are no girls – they have left the area.
- It is obvious that Tim likes being with the other children and that he enjoys this type of play.
- Another child has now got the brush and Tim joins forces with another to try to get the brush back.
- During this observation, Tim shows that he is a social child and he enjoys the activity or game if other children are involved. If he wants something, he does not get aggressive but is persistent.

In many ways, this method of using a framework to evaluate a child's development in one particular area is reminiscent of the approach of learning stories (Carr, 2001). When assessing babies and young children, it is valuable to be able to look at their development over time as it is only over a period of time that you can see how the holistic nature of children's learning and development is interwoven. Practitioners frequently describe their collection of observations as a learning story or learning journey. In this instance, to be purist and to follow strands of children's learning through time along a particular path gives a deeper and clearer understanding of how that baby or child is developing. In Chapter 5, Case study 24, it is clear from the observations of Sam that his early interest in turning pages using his fine motor skills is transferred to his control of the Game Boy and in turn this is transferred to his ability to use and manipulate writing tools with accuracy and precision, and ultimately this results in a child of 3 years of age being able to operate and navigate a computer program using a mouse control. This is a true learning story as it narrates Sam's journey of development in fine motor control.

Figures 7.2 and 7.3 (pp. 132–3) illustrate how, in using the approach of Carr (2001), a framework for a learning story can be created and used to inform how a baby is learning in one particular area of development.

Carr discusses how a child's learning can be assessed using the following criteria:

- taking an interest
- being involved
- persisting with difficulty
- expressing an idea or a feeling
- taking responsibility.

The two case study learning journeys show how an observation can be assessed to identify next steps within a particular area of development. The second learning story is the observation of Sam's play with the treasure basket which we looked at in Case study 3.

The frameworks offered give practitioners the opportunity to reflect on their practice as well as giving the basis for future learning and development of individual children.

Reflections

This book has considered all of the elements that need to be present in the environment when supporting babies and young children in a range of settings. If we are to support young children to become capable learners and have good levels of emotional wellbeing, we need to have regard to the quality of our practice and work with a true understanding or our own ethos and philosophy. Our starting point should always be to have an understanding and knowledge of what has gone before so that we can truly reflect on the ideas of the past and move them forwards to have meaning in our society today. When we can understand that the theorists and the pioneers of the past have influenced and moulded our practice, then we understand how we can adapt and challenge that practice. We also need to have an awareness of the policy of different governments because it is these which inevitably impact on how we care for babies and young children.

We live in an age where policies are changing but if you reflect back on history, it can be seen that the philosophies of the past are still relevant today. In fact, as previously mentioned, it is worrying that we have not moved that far since the days of the McMillan sisters and their innovative programmes to move children out of poverty to offer them structures for their future learning.

Having got to where we are, it is incumbent upon us to continually challenge ourselves and to reflect on our practice. Now that some

Learning Story		
Taking an interest	Lynda asks the adult 'Can I have a go in a minute?' She is so interested that the adult makes space for her at the table and she immediately becomes engaged in what she is doing.	
Being involved	She is interested and engaged.	
Persisting with difficulty	Lynda is not happy when the adult tells her friend to move round the table where there is more space. He moves but he soon returns to stand next to Lynda as she makes space to accommodate him.	
Expressing an idea or a feeling	Lynda tells the adult what she is doing – I am rolling a ball. As she speaks, Lynda uses intonation and gesture – nodding her head and tilting her head to one side. She now talks about making two eyes. Lynda sometimes takes on a motherly role, ensuring that her friend has all the dough that he needs.	Photographs illustrating the child's journey can be placed here
Taking responsibility	A child arrives at nursery and Lynda greets him with excitement – she calls to him to come and join her at the table. He comes to stand next to her – as she has told him. She shares the dough with him. She tells him 'Don't drop it on the floor, play with it'. When the two children go off to look at books together, Lynda can be seen trying to make sure that her friend is OK before they settle down.	

Short-term Review	What Next?
Question: What learning did I think went on here (i.e. the main point(s) of the learning story)?	*Questions: How might we encourage this interest, ability, strategy, disposition, story to:*
• Lynda shows that she is the leader in this relationship. She obviously gets great pleasure from it. The relationship shows Lynda's growing emotional security – she has always been confident but this bonding with another child shows that she is 'growing up'. • Lynda clearly understands the concept of sharing and showing concern for others.	• *be more complex?* • *appear in different areas of activities in the programme?* *How might we encourage the next 'step' in the learning story framework?* To encourage this growing socialization, especially when her special friend is not there, create situations where Lynda can play, share and turn take with a larger group of children.

Figure 7.2 Case study of a learning story 1: Lynda

Learning Story		
Taking an interest	Sam studies the basket and there is a change in his activity. His breathing and his arm movements are much more defined. He doesn't like the touch of the loofah fish – the touch puts him off.	
Being involved	Sam reaches in to the basket and begins to engage with a wide range of the resources – the scarf, the spoons which he returns to again and again, the shells and the brushes. He likes to look at himself in the reflecting plate and use the spoons to make a noise. He holds them up and really explores and investigates them. He is absorbed and is rarely distracted, other than when he hits himself on the head.	Photographs illustrating the child's journey can be placed here
Persisting with difficulty	When some of the resources have rolled to the other side of the basket, Sam presses on the edge of the basket several times until eventually the resource he wants rolls towards him. He repeats this action until he can finally grasp the object.	
Expressing an idea or a feeling	There is a pace with which he is touching the things in the basket.	
Taking responsibility	He looks for approval when he discovers that the resources will roll to him.	

Short-term Review	**What Next?**
(Question: What learning did I think went on here i.e. the main point(s) of the learning story)?	*Questions: How might we encourage this interest, ability, strategy, disposition, story to:*
• Sam showed good levels of concentration and involvement with the treasure basket. • Sam showed that he can persist even when there are problems. • Sam showed an interest in the shiny metal plate when selecting resources from the basket – he returned to this to look into it and to bang it with other objects.	• *be more complex?* • *appear in different areas of activities in the programme?* *How might we encourage the next 'step' in the learning story framework?* • Provide more opportunities for Sam to engage with open-ended resources. • Possibly assemble a basket which is made up of objects to look into and those which will make a noise when banged against one another.

Figure 7.3   Case study of a learning story 2: Sam

children are spending large parts of their early lives in out-of-home care, we need to continually reflect on how we adapt our environments to meet their needs. The chapter on emotional environments stresses the importance of getting this right for babies and young children from the start. The work of Field (2010) and Allen (2011) has set the emotional wellbeing of babies and children as one of their priorities, which is evident in the Early Intervention programme. If we can create caring and challenging environments for babies and young children, we are giving them that early intervention.

In amongst all of the work that we do with babies and young children, we as adults also need to ensure that we challenge ourselves professionally so that we can offer those in our care the learning that they as individuals need. The coalition government has rightly recognized the importance of having highly qualified practitioners to work with our youngest children, but in my opinion this will always be a struggle whilst they remain an unrecognized profession with regard to pay and conditions. With increasing professionalism, the status of those working with our very youngest children will be raised. Recchia and Shin (2010) looked at practitioners' views of working with children under 3 and found that their training had predominately concentrated on children over 3 years of age. This gap in training means that '… what students know about infancy often remains theoretical, academic and superficial'. Recchia and Shin found that training for the under 3s has less of a status than that given to those working with older children, thus creating a divide between 'teachers' and 'caregivers'. It is only when this matter is addressed that babies and young children will be supported by practitioners with a high level of qualification and professionalism. This can only mean a raising of the quality of care and learning that we give to the youngest children in our care.

At the heart of all the work that we do in early years is our role in partnership with parents. Research (EPPE; Mathers and Sylva, 2007; Mathers et al., 2007; Field, 2010; Allen, 2011) has highlighted the importance of the home learning environment. It is our role to support, rather than to judge, parents. We need to ensure that when we talk of partnership with parents we mean it. It also has to be recognized that, in many cases, this is a very hard task as some parents do not see the link between the home and the setting. We have to make sure that we endeavour to cement this partnership and forge these links. Part of our role is not only to challenge those practitioners who think that babies only require care but also to challenge the perception of adults caring for babies outside of the setting that this is the most important time in a child's life as it is in these crucial early years that the foundations for all future learning are laid.

One of our major roles in developing this partnership is sharing with parents what we know about their children. We do this through our observations of how babies and young children play and learn. These observations have to be relevant, not just pieces of paper for an Ofsted inspection. They need to be used so that we can reflect on what babies and young children are interested in and where they are at in their learning. I would recommend that as part of this reflection on our observations we as practitioners need to be self-critical. I have found that those who have taken part in the Every Child a Talker programme and used video cameras to observe the children and their own practice, have greatly improved their understanding of the children, as well as having a new insight into their work. Practitioners have commented on how they have adapted their interactions after having seen themselves on a video.

The framework offered is a starting point to raise practitioners' awareness of what is happening in their settings. It can be used in a range of ways to reflect on interaction, the environment, practice and the experiences of babies and young children.

In conclusion, caring for babies and young children is both a challenging and rewarding job. It is important that we get it right for those young children in our care. They and their families rely on us to offer them high quality experiences through high quality environments.

 Questions for reflection

- Reflect on the suggested framework for observation. How could you use it within your work: to observe young children, to observe practitioners or to evaluate what experiences are available for babies and young children?
- How could you develop a system for learning stories which could follow a child's journey as he travels from room to room in your setting?

Further reading

Harms, T., Clifford, R.M. and Cryer, D. (2003) *Infant/Toddler Environmental Rating Scale Revised (ITERS-R)*. Teachers College Press.
This is the environmental audit for children under the age of 3. It gives the scale points which an accredited assessor would use in order to conduct the audit.

Miller, L. and Pound, L. (eds) (2011) *Theories and Approaches to Learning in the Early Years*. London: Sage.
This book gives an overview of and introduction to the theories and research within early years.

Recchia, S. and Shin, M. (2010) 'Baby Teachers': How Pre-service Early Childhood Students Transform their Conceptions of Teaching and Learning through an Infant Practicum. *Early Years*, 30 (2): 135–45.
This journal article explores the challenges for those practitioners new to working with babies and very young children. It explores changes to their practices and challenges their pre-conceived ideas about working with this age group.

References

Allen, G. (2011) Early Intervention: The Next Steps. Available at: http://preventionaction.org/sites/all/files/Early%20intervention%20report.pdf

Carr, M. (2001) *Assessment in Early Childhood Settings: Learning Stories.* London: Paul Chapman Publishing.

Department for Education and Skills (DfES) (2002) *Birth to Three Matters.* Nottingham: DfES Publications.

Department for Education and Skills (DfES) (2007) *Statutory Framework for the Early Years Foundation Stage: Setting the Standards for Learning, Development and Care for Children from Birth to Five.* Nottingham: DfES Publications.

Field, F. (2010) *The Foundation Years: Preventing Poor Children Becoming Poor Adults.* London: Cabinet Office.

Harms, T., Clifford, R.M. and Cryer, D. (2003) *Infant/Toddler Environmental Rating Scale Revised (ITERS-R).* Teachers College Press.

Mathers, S. and Sylva, K. (2007) *National Evaluation of the Neighbourhood Nurseries Initiative: The Relationship between Quality and Children's Behavioural Development.* Nottingham: DfES Publications.

Mathers, S., Sylva, K. and Joshi, H. (2007) *Quality of Childcare Settings in the Millennium Cohort Study.* Nottingham: DfES Publications.

Recchia, S. and Shin, M. (2010) 'Baby Teachers': How Pre-service Early Childhood Students Transform their Conceptions of Teaching and Learning through an Infant Practicum. *Early Years,* 30 (2): 135–45.

Sylva, K., Siraj-Blatchford, I. and Taggart, B. (2004) *The Effective Provision of Pre-School Provision (EPPE Project): Final Report.* Nottingham: DfES Publications.

Sylva, K., Siraj-Blatchford, I. and Taggart, B. (2006) *Assessing Quality in the Early Years: Early Childhood Environment Rating Scale (ECERS-E).* Stoke-on-Trent: Trentham Books.

Tickell, C. (2011) *The Early Years: Foundations for Life, Health and Learning.* London: DfE. Available at www.education.gov.uk/tickellreview

Index

CREATIVITY IN THE PRIMARY CLASSROOM

Juliet Desailly *Education Consultant*

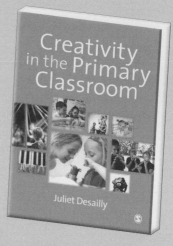

'This book deepens and broadens our understandings of creativity as applied to primary education. It provides a balance of practical frameworks and approaches with wise guidance. Many schools and individual teachers will find Juliet Desailly's work invaluable as they embrace the greater pedagogical and curricular freedoms promised by government.' *- Jonathan Barnes, Senior lecturer in Primary Education at Canterbury Christ Church University.*

Creativity is an integral element of any primary classroom. It has been never more important for teachers to involve children in their own learning and provide a curriculum that motivates and engages. Being creative involves generating new ideas, reflecting upon and evaluating different teaching approaches, and establishing an environment that supports creativity.

Creativity in the Primary Classroom explores how to develop as a creative teacher and how to foster creativity in your classes. Drawing from key literature and detailed real-life examples, Juliet Desailly puts into practice her extensive experience planning, advising and developing creative approaches to teaching and curriculum planning.

This book examines what creativity in a primary classroom can look like, and is supported throughout by practical activities for use across curriculum subjects and reflective tasks encouraging critical engagement with key conceptual issues.

This is essential reading for students on primary initial teacher education courses including undergraduate (BEd, BA with QTS), postgraduate (PGCE, SCITT), and employment-based routes into teaching, and also for practicing teachers wishing to enhance their own teaching.

CONTENTS

Section One: What is Creativity? \ The Key Elements of Creativity \ Creativity in Education: History and Theoretical Background \ PART TWO: A CREATIVE CHILD IN A CREATIVE CLASSROOM \ Building the Skills to Work Creatively \ Establishing the Ethos \ PART THREE: A CREATIVE TEACHER \ What Makes a Creative Teacher? \ Key Skills for the Creative Teacher \ PART FOUR: A CREATIVE CURRICULUM \ Planning for Creative Outcomes \ Medium Term Planning for Creative Outcomes \ Case Studies: Creativity in Practice

READERSHIP

This is essential reading for Students on primary initial teacher education courses, as well as practicing teachers wishing to enhance their own teaching

March 2012 • 176 pages
Cloth (978-0-85702-763-4) • £60.00 / Paper (978-0-85702-764-1) • £19.99

ALSO AVAILABLE FROM SAGE

RISK AND ADVENTURE IN EARLY YEARS OUTDOOR PLAY

Learning from Forest Schools

Sara Knight *Anglia Ruskin University*

Do you want to create exciting outdoor experiences for children? Are you looking for guidance on how to incorporate the wilder and riskier elements of outdoor play into your planning?

This book will give you the confidence to offer the children in your setting adventurous and challenging outdoor activities, as well as ways to utilize natural resources to their best advantage. There is clear, practical advice on what you need to do, which is underpinned by the theory that supports the benefits of this approach. Examples from settings are included, to illustrate best practice and to show how things can be achieved.

Issues considered include:

- being outside in bad weather
- the importance of risk-taking
- the benefits of rough-and-tumble play
- observing and assessing children in this mode
- how these experiences improve children's learning
- explaining activities to parents, colleagues and managers
- ensuring health and safety requirements are met
- the role of the adult in facilitating these experiences.

Suitable for all students and practitioners working with young children from birth to eight years , this book will not only give you ideas for outdoor play but also help you understand exactly what you are doing, why it is educationally sound and developmentally important for children, and where it connects with the Early Years Foundation Stage in England, the Foundation Phase in Wales and the Curriculum for Excellence in Scotland .

April 2011 • 152 pages
Cloth (978-1-84920-629-7) • £60.00
Paper (978-1-84920-630-3) • £19.99

ALSO FROM SAGE

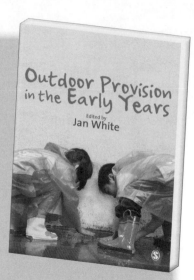